THE**VEGAN**MONOLOGUES

THEVEGANMONOLOGUES

COLLECTED ESSAYS

BENSHABERMAN

APPRENTICEHOUSE
BALTIMOREMARYLAND

Library of Congress Cataloging-in-Publication Data

Shaberman, Ben
    The vegan monologues : collected essays /
Ben Shaberman.
        p. cm.
    ISBN 978-1-934074-36-7
    1. American wit and humor. I. Title.

PN6165.S457 2008
814'.54--dc22
                            2008027234

Printed in the United States of America

First Edition

Published by Apprentice House
The Future of Publishing...Today!

Apprentice House
Communication Department
Loyola College in Maryland
4501 N. Charles Street
Baltimore, MD 21210

410.617.5265
www.ApprenticeHouse.com
info@ApprenticeHouse.com

For Samson, Delilah, Chester, Woody, and Gandhi

For Samson, Delilah, Chester, Woody, and Gandhi

"It's the same with men as with horses and dogs.
Nothing wants to die."
Tom Waits
"The Fall of Troy"

TABLEOFCONTENTS

INTRODUCTION

It all started with a stool.

In 1989, I ordered a two-piece vanity for my then-fiancée as a Hanukkah gift. However, when I went to pick it up from the furniture maker, it wasn't finished being built. Only the accompanying stool was ready. So I decided to bring just the stool to her family's party and keep the rest of the gift as a mystery. I knew she really wanted a vanity and might figure out that the stool belonged to one. Even if she didn't figure it out, I thought she'd be thrilled to learn in another week that the stool went with a vanity. "I love you, you're wonderful honey!" she would shout when I presented her with the other half of the present. I would be treated to wild, steamy sex in appreciation for my incredibly thoughtful and generous gift.

Well, my then-fiancée — let's call her "Agatha" to protect her true identity — never figured out what the stool was for and was infuriated that I wouldn't tell her. I was in deep stool. There would never be any steamy sex — only the threat of testicular rearrangement without anesthesia. I have to admit that Agatha's two younger brothers and I delighted in teasing and taunting her about the mystery stool, and her escalating torment only spurred us on.

Agatha and I were supposed to get married on 7-8-90, which I thought was pretty cool, numerically speaking. But our engagement was officially called off on the far less remarkable date of 6-24-90. Canceling a wedding that was only two weeks away — and it was to be a big Jewish extravaganza at the local Hyatt — set a new personal record for embarrassment for me. (That record would remain unbroken until 2000 when I moved to Iowa to be with a woman I met on the Internet. Read about it on page 47.)

The wedding debacle made me realize that I was not cut out for a domesticated lifestyle nor could I ever take life too seriously again. It's not that I decided never to give a crap about anything — in fact I think I care more now than I ever did — but rather I chose not to look too far ahead. Part of the problem I had with marriage is that it caused me to look forty or fifty years into the future and that scared the bejeezus out of me. And, there would be the responsibilities of a wife, kids, a house, and all that keeping up with the Joneses.

So, over the next few years, I decided to simplify and downsize my life. I gave up my job at IBM (and the big salary), gave up meat, gave up furniture, gave up television, and did the most obvious thing a person with two computer science degrees would do during the height of the dot.com boom — I got a poetry degree.

Poetry was cool. I enjoyed studying clever and humorous poets like Howard Nemerov, E.E. Cummings, and Elizabeth Bishop. And, it was fun to try my own hand at writing verse.

While at the Sewanee Writers' Conference in 1994, I had the distinct honor of having my poetry critiqued by Anthony Hecht (1923-2004) — a world-renowned master of blank verse and former U.S. Poet Laureate. Considering that Tony was a man of words, he had surprisingly little to say about my work — mainly because of its lack of meter and structure. He basically said it wasn't poetry. I'm guessing that Tony — like my ex-fiancée — wouldn't have appreciated my stool mystery game either.

For me, the problem with poetry is that no one reads it. The only people who do are other poets, and there aren't a whole lot of poets roaming the Earth.

Fast forward a few years later and a particularly sobering trip to the doctor inspired "The Further Adventures of Eczema Boy" — an essay that appeared as a health section cover story in *The Washington Post*. A bad breakout provided me with my first literary breakthrough. (Grab some moisturizer and go read the article on page 81.)

Since then, I've had the good fortune of having had many of my essays run in a lot of well-known and not-so-well-known publications. I am thrilled whenever a piece is published, because I know somebody out there is reading it.

One other note for the record: My editor, Gregg Wilhelm, came up with the catchy title, *The Vegan Monologues*, because many of the essays in the book have some connection to my veganish ways. I have to admit, Gregg's pretty clever for a carnivore.

PARTONE

THAT CAT WAS A BREATH OF FRESH AIR. ACHOO!

Appeared in The Washington Post *(November 15, 2004)*

Just because I'm a vegetarian doesn't mean I like pets. What's the fun in creatures that smell, scratch, bite, and occasionally make unwanted sexual advances?

Actually, for me, the worst thing about pets is my allergies to them. When I was a kid I suffered frequently because my family was always visiting relatives with cats and dogs. So my vegetarianism and compassion for creatures has been more of an academic thing. I could go on and on about the moral, environmental and health virtues of a meat-free lifestyle. However, unlike many of my vegetarian pals who absolutely adore their cats and dogs, I am blissfully pet-free.

My vegan girlfriend, Jeannie, is a lover of *all* animals, including injured foxes, groundhogs and squirrels left on the side of the highway. Jeannie handles wild critters as if they were her own children. Never before have I had to worry about picking up rabies in an intimate relationship.

Because of my allergies, I was not pleased when I learned that Jeannie had two cats. It's no fun to make out when you're a drippy, sneezy, allergic mess. But I really like Jeannie — I've fallen in love with her — so I decided to do my best to tolerate her dander-laden feline roommates, Samson and Delilah. It's not as though Samson and Delilah had a strong affection for me either, in the beginning, taking refuge under the bed whenever I'd come over.

After a few visits, though, Delilah mustered up enough courage to come out from hiding, especially if I was lugging a bag of aromatic takeout Chinese food. When there are eats around she meows loudly and persistently, "Supersize me." She is one fat cat.

But the frail, black and bony, sixteen-year-old Samson remained in seclusion for many more weeks. That is, until his health took a turn for the worse. We knew his progressing kidney disease would mean the end for him soon. Surprisingly, during his decline, Samson began to come out from hiding. He was no longer afraid of me, and eventually allowed me to pet him. We developed a new understanding — cat to man — which neither of us ever envisioned.

Despite his frail condition, Samson was still a beautiful cat with hypnotic green eyes and cute little fangs. And he became a mellow cat, with a cool, steady stride. Nothing much bothered him anymore — not even my loud and persistent sneezing.

I was happy to assist with Samson's health care. Jeannie had me help administer his subcutaneous fluids, and I began making trips to the vet with them. In my forty-three years, I never thought I'd ever set foot in a vet's office — the equivalent of purgatory for a pet-allergy sufferer like me.

Samson hung on for a few months. He could have been a poster cat for Medicare with all his medications and medical bills, but he was okay. And though I visited Jeannie's house to visit Jeannie, I always made it a point to hang out with Samson and scratch him on the back of his head. (Of course, I'd wash my hands thoroughly afterward, and take a puff on the old inhaler.) Inevitably, Samson's condition deteriorated to the point where he had to be euthanized. That cold and dreary evening was one of the saddest of my life. Jeannie was devastated. Even Delilah, who never seemed to pay attention to her brother, was notably disturbed by his absence. The three of us were a collective wreck.

But my grief for Samson was indicative of a newfound appreciation for animals. What's most remarkable to me is that when faced with his own mortality, he transformed into a courageous and loving cat. He passed on quite gracefully.

I was so inspired and impressed by Samson, I decided to take my vegetarianism to a new level and become a vegan, forsaking all animal products (e.g., milk and eggs). What better way to honor my unlikely friend and hero?

I'll never be like Jeannie, combing the roadside for injured or abandoned animals. Nor does it appear that my allergies to animals are going to miraculously disappear. But it is nice to know that I — along with the rest of the animal-human kingdom — am capable of more compassion than I imagine, despite formidable barriers and obstacles. Just don't take away my inhaler.

UNAVOIDABLE BUMPS — AND BUMPERS — IN THE ROAD

Appeared in The Washington Post *(January 21, 2008)*

Nothing says you're pathetic quite like losing your bumper in the middle of traffic — except maybe the act of retrieving said bumper while onlookers, sitting comfortably in their shiny SUVs and late-model sports cars, stare at you in complete awe.

I lost my bumper after hitting the edge of a curb. Though I heard a loud clank upon the impact, I figured that was just the jack bouncing around in my trunk. Imagine my surprise when I saw my bumper in my rear-view mirror as I drove away. By the time I figured out what was going on, I was beginning to cross a bridge — a very unsafe place to stop my car. Yet, I knew my bumper was blocking traffic. I decided to proceed across the span — bewildered and bumperless. Once I was over, I parked off to the side, and hustled on foot back across the bridge to claim my car's posterior appendage.

Fortunately, some good Samaritan had moved the bumper to the sidewalk, so that it didn't cause any further traffic problems. I feel bad for the person who did the deed, because the old hunk of rubber and metal was covered in some sure-to-be-toxic soot and dust.

As I began my Walk of Shame — trudging back over the bridge with bumper in hand — I wondered if it was time to give up on my white '89 Volvo 240, which had racked up more than 225,000 miles. The average Vespa has a higher book value than that car, but like many ancient Volvo 240s, it still runs great. And, investing in a new car reduces the amount of money I can put toward retirement. I'm only forty-six years old, but with Medicare and Social Security hurdling toward extinction, and the cost of health care sky rocketing, I'll need retirement savings of about $9 million to maintain my modest standard of living. I'll need even more of a nest egg if my vegan lifestyle translates into longevity.

What also came to mind during that five-minute trek with my detachable bumper was how much I had grown to dislike our automobile-driven society. It's amazing how our cars have gotten bigger and more costly at a time when oil dependence is creating so many enormous economic, political, and environmental problems.

I began imagining what it would be like if we all drove Smart Cars, or hybrids, or just any car that got a minimum of forty miles per gallon. What if we took the savings from lower fuel expenditures, lower insurance premiums, smaller car payments, and cleaner air, and invested it in education for our kids, or health care for the elderly and underserved, or a $9 million retirement fund for me?

By the time I reached my car, which was waiting patiently to have its bumper reattached, I was feeling better about myself and my frugal choice of transportation. Sure my old Volvo wasn't perfect — I wish it got better than twenty-five miles per gallon — but it's a lot less wasteful than many cars out there. My Walk of Shame had become a Walk of Hope. I found myself humming "We've Only Just Begun." I was beaming like Richard Simmons at a weight-loss reunion.

The best news to come out of that whole ordeal was that my trusty, independent mechanic, Han, was able to hook me up with a used — i.e., recycled — bumper from a junkyard for $150.

Though my new bumper gave me hope of taking my Volvo to 300,000 miles and beyond, it was not to be. At the 235,000 mile mark, I learned a new automotive lesson: Losing a bumper isn't nearly as pathetic as having your car catch on fire in front of your place of employment at the height of evening rush hour.

The incident happened as I was leaving my office parking lot. The first hint of trouble was when the car stalled. I was able to start it right back up, but only made it a few yards before it conked out on me again.

Then came the plumes of smoke from underneath the hood. Then came my hurried search for any valuable items before I evacuated. Then came me, standing in a cloud of smoke, directing traffic around my burning car. Then came the police and fire department. Then came my co-workers — Angie, Mitsy, Linda, and Dorie — driving by on their way home for the evening. I'm not sure what proper car-fire etiquette is, but they were all very willing to give me a ride or help in anyway they could.

Frankly, this was the most excitement I'd had since someone brought a dish made with chicken stock to a vegan potluck.

I must admit, I was hoping to see my car just burst into flames. I'm not an arsonist nor do I seek out mass destruction, but I am a guy and even we compassionate men have a little bit of pyromaniac tucked away in the recesses of our crowded minds.

Though there was significant damage under the hood, and the car was later deemed "totaled," there was never the explosive drama I had hoped for. I did, however, get $751 from my insurance company for the loss of the vehicle. It's not quite enough for a new hybrid, but a respectable sum nonetheless.

About a week after "The Great Fire," I paid a visit to the local junkyard to claim a few items out of the trunk of my car — a snow shovel, boots, and a portable radio. It was sad to see my old Volvo in a muddy field among the piles of twisted and rusting car frames. This really was the end of the road.

However, I do take consolation in the fact that I kept that Volvo going for so long. It outlasted three computers, three careers, and four relationships. If I am lucky, maybe a bumper or wheel from it will live on as a replacement part for a 240 owned by some other conservation-oriented person like me. With the huge cost of retirement, used auto parts just might be the highlight of my legacy.

HOW I BECAME A TAKEOUT JUNKIE

Appeared in VegNews *(September-October 2006)*

I was in a pathetic state when it all began — grief-stricken and roach-stricken. It was 1990, and I had just split up with my fiancée and moved out of her place into a buggy Washington, D.C., studio apartment. Actually the breakup wasn't all that bad; we'd been driving each other crazy for months, and were ready to part ways. Parting with the roaches was not so easy.

Though I'd always been drawn to the traffic, crime, and noise of urban living, I'd had enough of the resilient creepy crawlers. In other dwellings, I had tried everything to purge roaches — sprays, traps, exterminators, roach motels, roach timeshares — but nothing worked. It's amazing how little adversity it takes for two human beings to leave one another, yet roaches stick around even after being doused with toxic chemicals and getting whacked over the head with shoes, brooms, and newspapers.

So this time around, I decided on a different approach to roach elimination. I made my kitchen food-free. What roach in its right mind would hang out in my barren place when every other unit was well-stocked with eats?

With all the markets, coffeehouses and restaurants within walking distance, I just ran out when I got hungry. It wasn't the cheapest way to go, but I considered the luxury of outsourcing my meals to be part of my post-relationship therapy.

The biggest challenge was deciding what to order — the options were many and flavorful: Chinese, Lebanese, Thai, and Indian. As a vegetarian, I ate a ton of vegetables, rice, beans, and tofu. Binging on Asian and Middle Eastern food is nothing like the fatalistic "Supersize Me" regimen. In fact, eating foreign cuisines can be quite healthy. And, keeping food out of the house made it less convenient to indulge in late-night snacking; a zero inventory of food is not a bad way to stay slim and trim.

Unfortunately, the roaches never left. But getting carry-out food all the time was pure decadence. Every meal was freshly prepared and delicious, and there was no cooking and minimal cleanup. I never read Sir Thomas More's classic story, *Utopia*, but I bet there was a whole chapter about ordering carryout.

I've been a takeout junkie now for fifteen years. Sure I've had lapses and cooked up an occasional instant oatmeal or canned soup, but I've kept my to-go habit going strong while living in a variety of locales, including Des Moines, Miami, and now Baltimore.

I do feel guilty sometimes about my bloated food budget, but when I look at the money people spend on cars, homes, clothes, vacations, and jewelry, I don't find my habit that indulgent. Furthermore, I often buy my carryout meals from family-owned establishments; I'm giving my business to everyday people just like myself. When I consider the thousands I shell out annually in federal taxes that go for invading other countries, ordering carryout seems pretty inconsequential. In fact, we might be getting a better response in Iraq if we had brought more Szechwan stir fry and less shock and awe.

Unfortunately, though, takeout food can't cure all the world's problems. It didn't end my roach infestation, and I'm sure it wouldn't have held my engagement together. But at least now when I head home at the end of the day lugging those ubiquitous white cartons with the wire handles, I'm pretty content. And if my persistent roommates are snatching errant morsels of my culinary treasures, at least they're going vegan.

OFF THE WARPATH

Appeared in Vegetarian Times *(October 2006)*

We vegetarians are a righteous lot. Despite the fact that about 97 percent of the U.S. population eats animals, we the meat-free minority are convinced that we're right and the carnivorous majority is wrong. And, there is not a vegetarian out there who hasn't tried to convert a murderous meat-munching heathen. We use all sorts of seemingly indisputable and obvious arguments — citing strong moral, environmental, and health examples — when we're proselytizing. Yet, at the conclusion of our rants, we usually hear something lame like, "I just need my meat." It's a baffling phenomenon.

I'm not exactly a zealot, but I do believe my vegan diet is a better way to live, and over the years, I myself have tried to persuasively plead my case to friends, family, and coworkers. After failing miserably time after time to make any progress, I began my quest for the perfect argument — a case so compelling, no one with a conscience could ignore its validity.

Enter my cannibalism theory. It goes like this: When we were prehistoric humans, cannibalism was commonplace. It was the one source of sustenance you could count on. Talk about convenience food. Just conk someone on the head while they're sleeping, and you and your family were well fed for days. "How about we dine on one of the Johnsons tonight? I could really go for a meaty thigh."

But then, one of these cave people became sad, because they were "running out" of friends. So they decided to try eating an animal instead. They even learned how to prepare the animal so it tasted just like a human. "Honey, is this antelope or one of the Dickersons? I can't tell the difference!" And so began a new evolutionary period. Maybe it took centuries or even millennia, but eventually cannibalism became a dining experience of the past. My point was that we are again at a key evolutionary moment, and the more progressive, forward-thinking people are now moving away from eating animals and going toward vegetarianism.

It didn't take long to figure out that this was not a stroke of public relations genius. Cannibalism references do nothing but cause people to think about plane crash survival stories and primitive tribes with large ornaments hanging from their nostrils — it's not the stuff of dietary epiphanies.

So over the past few years, I decided to just give up initiating conversations about vegetarianism. It had become a futile exercise. I had burned out on explaining all the hows and whys. My meatless diet only came up when I ordered food, and I needed to make sure that I would get an appropriate meal.

What I began to find is that the more passive I was about my animal-free lifestyle, the more people wanted to know. They were curious about what I ate, where I ate, how I got my protein, and if I missed meat. If they asked me why I was a vegan, I usually said something simple like, "I prefer not to eat animals or animal products." When it came to fully exposing my feelings about being a vegan, I was playing hard to get. I discovered that my muted meat-free persona attracted more attention.

What's most heartening is that my coworkers, a traditionally dismissive group, now go out of their way to make sure I get vegan food at parties, retreats, and other events. They seem to enjoy the process — it's become a mission for them. And what's most gratifying for me is that they're learning about vegetarianism through their own actions. Even though they aren't going meat-free themselves, at least they're participating in my meatless world.

Maybe some time in the future, because of a health issue or an encounter with a suffering animal, one of these friends or colleagues will make the leap to vegetarianism, or at least dare to try some tofu. Maybe because of what they learned while accommodating me, they'll see it's not so radical. But I learned that I can't make the leap for them.

A final point of clarification: That cannibalism shtick was not only a lousy idea, it simply wasn't true. Yes, the practice of eating one's peers did exist, but after doing some research, I discovered that it wasn't as pervasive as I made it out to be. So, I am guilty of creating a little historical propaganda. No harm done. But I have to admit, I feel the same compulsion to spin hyperbolic claims and slogans that corporate advertising gurus must feel. I can hear it now — the catchy cannibalism commercial with a voice over by Anthony Hopkins: "Dave in accounting — the other white meat."

A VEGAN EATS NOTHING BUT
CHINESE TAKEOUT FOR THIRTY DAYS

As I gaze out over the salad bar at my local "wholesome food" chain store, I become frustrated and depressed. The spinach is wilted. The broccoli and carrot bins are empty. Many of the pre-made concoctions are suspended in an unidentifiable, cream-colored, congealed goo. The smells emanating from the station suggest biology experiment rather than dining experience. I had already passed by the deli counter, where there were so many meat, pork, and poultry options on display, I felt as though I was visiting a farm-animal memorial park; the pickings were slim for a meat-free guy like me.

In my hour of dietary darkness, I decide it's time to embark on a culinary journey that I'd been pondering for many months. Tomorrow, I will begin eating nothing but Chinese food for the next thirty days.

Gastronomically speaking, I will be coming to Jesus, or in my case, Buddha. (No crucifixion, just cruciferous vegetables.) Why continue to suffer through the evil and perversion of the fallen American food industry? As restaurants and grocery stores have become bigger business, the quality and nutritional value of food has gone down the crapper. As I've mentioned already, even the so-called healthy places have their issues. I would much rather buy my eats from family-owned operations — from people who want to make fresh, flavorful food and a decent living rather than solely trying to maximize the value of their stock. The average American gut is a testament to the slop that the corporations are feeding us, and we're gladly stuffing away. Our society is becoming so large, it's difficult to distinguish the livestock from the consumer.

Admittedly, my Chinese-only plan doesn't involve much martyrdom or hardship. Unlike the guy in the movie *Supersize Me* who ate nothing but McDonald's for a month, I'm not a masochist. Make no mistake about it, I love Chinese food. I've been getting Chinese takeout three to five times a week for years. I got hooked on the stuff back in the '60s when I was a kid. My dad loved to take me to Chung Wah's, a dive under an old railroad bridge in Cleveland's inner city. Not only did they have the best won ton soup in town, we might even catch a drunken fist fight in the parking lot, if we were lucky. Those were the good old "chop suey, chow mein, one from column A, one from column B" days. Egg rolls and fried rice were exotic magical treats for me back then. As I got older, though, I developed a serious thing for egg foo yung, and began trying spicier Hunan and Szechwan alternatives that were coming to the States with the new influx of Chinese immigrants.

These days, my selections are usually healthy and always animal-free. My favorites include: stir-fried kale and yuba (chewy tofu skins), broccoli and tofu in garlic sauce, and moo shu vegetables (shredded cabbage, bean sprouts, and other light veggies wrapped in rice pancakes with tangy plum sauce). On special occasions, though, I might indulge in crispy seitan (wheat gluten) with walnuts — it's like a vegetarian version of Chicken McNuggets soaking in a hot orange sauce with the viscosity of 10W40 motor oil.

There is no authority or monitor watching me to see if I break my self-imposed, Chinese-only rules. I haven't thought long and hard about the technicalities, but I will allow myself to drink coffee, tea, and soda. I need the caffeine. I thought that I might need to drink orange juice for vitamin C, but my girlfriend, Jeannie, assured me that my scurvy risk was low. Despite her limited mobility due to a broken foot, Jeannie has agreed to be a part-time participant in my Chinese food-athon.

My venture will begin on August 9, which happens to be a rather dubious day in history. In 1974, President Nixon resigned because of the Watergate scandal. In 1969, the Manson family committed the Tate-Labianca murders. And in 1945, the U.S. dropped the A-bomb on Nagasaki. I guess it isn't too unreasonable to indulge in as much Chinese food as I can before our civilization completely self destructs.

Bring on the bok choy, baby!

WEEK ONE: *Let the games begin*

My first week involves many visits to Mr. Chan's. Their food is like vegetarian crack cocaine. I eat there two to three times a week even when I'm not doing this crazy Chinese diet. Chan's serves some amazingly tasty dishes with yuba, seitan, and textured vegetable protein, which very few restaurants — Chinese or otherwise — serve in Baltimore. These not-so-elegant-sounding meat alternatives are culinary jewels for vegetarians; they provide meat-like flavor and chewy texture without taking out any animals. (Just because I'm vegetarian doesn't mean I don't like the taste of meat.)

Chan's also serves brown rice, which is far more satisfying and nutritious than refined (white) rice. It holds moisture and flavor better than refined, making it a more tolerable leftover option, as well. I decide to order extra brown rice to last me for a few days.

I'm quickly establishing a rhythm: I buy two entrees in the evening. They cover me for dinner that night, breakfast the next day, and sometimes lunch.

Zip-a-dee-doo-dah

As I move through the first week of my dietary odyssey, one thing has become quite evident: The steady intake of Chinese food is like Liquid Plumber for my lower gastrointestinal system. I'd be the envy of Lawrence Welk fans everywhere. I guess the phenomenon is not surprising given the vast quantities of fibrous vegetables I'm ingesting three times a day.

Also, I've learned that cold leftover Chinese food for breakfast sucks; I feel as though I'm dining from Jeannie's backyard compost pile.

WEEK TWO: *GI Joe*

Let's just say I'm racking up a lot of frequent flusher points. I've actually lost a couple of pounds. I'm also a little low on energy. I've decided to go with more starch — vegetable-fried rice and chow fun noodles. Hopefully cutting back a bit on broccoli and kale — both are gastrointestinal rocket fuel — will slow things down.

I've really had a hankering for a bagel in the morning — that's been my biggest craving. The smell of popcorn at the movie theater has been driving me nuts, too.

It's amazing how wonderful a caffeinated cola (brand name purposely withheld) has been at the end of the day. There's always been something sublimely symbiotic about cola and Chinese food for me. Given that I'm not indulging in chocolate, cookies, or any of my usual late-evening treats, soda has become a highly appreciated staple in my daily diet.

WEEK THREE: *Trouble in paradise*

On Monday, Jeannie had some leftover napa from Tony Cheng's Szechwan House for lunch, and discovered FOUR SHRIMP in the takeout carton. For the record, in the vegetarian court of law, unknowingly eating an animal product is sort of like involuntary manslaughter.

We suspect that someone there didn't quite get the vegetarian concept and used shrimp in the dish. Or, the shrimp were remnants of a meal previously prepared in that pan. Regardless, as in so many Chinese or other ethnic restaurants, there's often a significant language barrier. Let me tell you, it's hard enough to get an English-speaking person to understand what vegetarian means. It's amazing how many people don't understand that fish and chicken are not vegetarian.

There was a happy ending to the shrimp fiasco. Jeannie's seventeen-year-old cat, Delilah, enjoyed the four errant crustaceans for a snack.

Also during the week, I suffered my first Chinese-food-related injury — chili pepper sauce in the eye. The culprit — Hunan Wok's Kung Pao tofu (hot and spicy with peanuts). I definitely experienced the Pao of that entrée. I felt like I lost a couple layers of my cornea. Still, the meal was quite tasty. I'm just considering protective eyewear from here on out.

WEEK FOUR: *Back on track*

I'm glad to report that I've regained control of my GI system. I felt that my Chinese-food dysentery was the one thing that could have derailed me from my outsourcing odyssey. I was running on empty.

My last week has been more of a moo shu vegetable and stir-fried string bean period. These options are not quite as "expressive" as they navigate my digestive tract, and they are quite ubiquitous throughout the Chinese restaurant community.

Chinese food for breakfast remains the biggest drag. Overnight in the fridge, the veggies go limp, the tofu goes mushy, and the sauce coagulates. It's like chow-mein-flavored Jello.

Indian food voyeur

After a movie (and lusting once again for popcorn) on a Sunday afternoon, Jeannie and I cruise upper suburban Baltimore looking for a new Chinese dining experience. However, many of the places we find are takeout, fortune-cookie-cutter operations. So many Chinese restaurants look and operate alike down to their menus, signs, murals, and fluorescent lighting. It's as if there's some underground operation in China cranking out these franchises. *Chinese Restaurant News* does in fact report that there are more Chinese restaurants in the U.S. (about 41,000) than McDonald's in the world (about 30,000). I guess capitalism can work well with a communist twist.

Anyway, in a moment of compassion, I decide to hang outdoors with Jeannie while she enjoys Aloo Mehti (potatoes and fenugreek) from Kathmandu, a favorite Indian-Nepalese eatery. It was time to show a little mercy. She's been a trooper through my wacky venture, gimping around from restaurant to restaurant in her protective boot, muttering expletives and references to the Americans with Disabilities Act.

Where do I go from here?

Though my Chinese-food odyssey has been a bit monotonous and inconvenient at times, I have mixed feelings about it coming to a close in a few days. Overall, I feel good, I'm trim, and my large intestine has reached a state of supreme enlightenment.

What's been remarkable to me about this diet is that as long as I go light on the oil, sauces, and rice, I can eat almost continuously. When I get full, I don't feel bloated, and within an hour or two, I'm ready for more.

Though I would enjoy the many non-fibrous things I've been missing — cookies, bagels, and chocolate — I don't want to upset the balance I've achieved.

Putting down my chopsticks

I enjoy mixed vegetables and fried rice from the Panda Gourmet for the final meal of my excursion. It's been a journey of seventy-five meals from eighteen predominantly Baltimore restaurants for a total cost of about $700.

I officially end my Chinese-only diet the next day by downing a pint of Vanilla Swiss Almond Rice Dream. As rather decadent dairy-free ice-cream-like frozen desserts, Rice Dream and Soy Dream are how we vegans practice dietary hedonism. I've been fantasizing about that pint of Rice Dream since day one of my venture.

Now that I am past my month-long experiment, I'm looking back on it as a culinary meditation. For thirty days, my diet was focused on a single cuisine. Though there was some diversity in what I ate, there was much that I didn't consume: no bread, bakery, fruit, or candy, and virtually nothing that was raw.

And what great epiphany did I experience?

Like any great adventurer — like those courageous folks who climb mountains, swim oceans, and navigate poles — I feel a sense of accomplishment. True, I didn't risk my life, but I did go to the edge, scatologically speaking.

But most of all, without exception, I enjoyed fresh, flavorful, and crispy vegetables for each and every meal. Sure, some restaurants did a better job with sauces, rice, and tofu. Chan's, for example, is in a class all by itself with their plethora of tasty meat alternatives. But it's clear that virtually all Chinese restaurants do vegetables well.

Chinese food can be unhealthy, if you aren't judicious about the sauces and deep frying. Many options can be oily and/or high in sodium. But for a vegetarian, or anyone who makes vegetables an important part of their diet, you can count on a Chinese eatery for an eclectic fix of quality vegetables including more unusual varieties like: bamboo shoots, mung bean sprouts, water chestnuts, napa, bok choy, and all sorts of tasty mushrooms.

And though the language barrier was sometimes a challenge, I found that almost all of these establishments would try — without complaint — to accommodate my special requests. Whether I asked for vegetarian sauce, tofu instead of meat, or extra broccoli, my servers pleasantly did their best to please.

Generally speaking, Chinese restaurant proprietors are not a gregarious or pretentious bunch. Their dining rooms — if they even have one — are usually decorated modestly. What's most impressive to me is that at many of the takeout restaurants, you can see the kitchen in action, making the orders from scratch in sizzling woks over iron stoves. Nothing's microwaved or pre-made.

Maybe what's most telling about my Chinese food experience is that I was back visiting Chan's and other neighborhood Chinese haunts just a few days after my month-long excursion ended. That's not to dismiss Indian, Thai, Vietnamese, or other vegetarian and vegetable-friendly cuisines that I enjoyed, as well. Rather it shows that I didn't burn out on Chinese. If anything, it upped my appreciation, and at the same time reinforced my discontent with most Western-style eating establishments.

I still shop at the local "wholesome food" chain store for bagels, Rice Dream, and household necessities. Occasionally, I take my chances at their salad bar or deli counter. But at the end of the day, I know I'm going to be satisfied getting a freshly made helping of Mr. Chan's stir-fried yuba and kale.

A final note: If you decide to embark on a vegetarian Chinese adventure like mine, always keep this lesser-known, ancient proverb in mind: He who walks through Buddha's garden will run to porcelain shrine.

REMEMBER WHEN WE SAW DAN RATHER?

I didn't exactly fall off my chair when my girlfriend, Jeannie, got an invitation to hear Dan Rather speak on President's Day in 2006. What came to mind was the bogus memo he unwittingly used to cast doubt on President Bush's service in the National Guard. Rather apologized for not verifying the memo's authenticity, but shortly thereafter, he resigned as anchor of the *CBS Evening News* — a position he held for twenty-four years.

Truth be told, I've never had strong opinions about Dan Rather. He's just been a persistently visible media figure that Baby Boomers like me have grown up, and old, with over the years.

Regardless of my ambivalence toward Rather, the event was free, and at the landmark Willard Hotel in Washington, D.C. Known as "the residence of presidents," the Willard is also where President Ulysses S. Grant coined the term "lobbyist" — a name he gave to people who sought favors from him while he relaxed in the lobby there.

Jeannie and I arrived unfashionably early to hear Rather, so we lounged on an exceedingly comfy couch in the opulent and expansive Willard lobby. Without large sums of cash, we weren't in a position to do much lobbying. So we just watched the affluent hotel guests, much more likely to dole out a bribe or a kickback, drift by. Efficient porters assisted the patrons with their luggage and questions about nearby dining options. A harpist played "Scarborough Fair." It was like we were in the credit card commercial where the final word of the voiceover is "priceless."

The Rather event was hosted by a marketing firm as a show of appreciation to their customers. Jeannie and I were more like friends of the customers. We didn't realize that cocktails and a plethora of hors d'ouerves would be served. They even had the proverbial slab of carved meat under an orange heating light. Waiters in tuxedos roamed around holding silver trays filled with shrimp and salmon concoctions. Too bad we're steadfast vegetarians. We shared a dinner roll. Eventually, the room filled up with 100 or so gregarious marketing professionals clad in well-tailored suits. I was glad that I had made the personal sacrifice of wearing a button-down shirt with a collar.

Rather arrived fashionably late for the event, but was quite gracious. He spoke with a mild Texas accent that gave him an endearing, folksy quality. He covered a lot of topical ground in his half-hour talk, with references to the rise of Islamic fundamentalism, growth of the Chinese and Indian economies, and the state of American media.

At a few different points during his talk, the veteran journalist rattled off the historical events he'd covered, as if he was naming the stops on a subway line: Kennedy, Martin Luther King, Vietnam, Watergate, the hostages in Iran. His nonchalance smacked more of humility than arrogance, and it was during those moments that I began to feel the weight of this man's experience.

There was one prophetic comment Rather made that really caught my attention. He said that the United States role as the world's only hyper-power — i.e., combined economic and military superpower — would not last forever, that our country's overwhelming superiority was just, as he called it, "a historical blip." Though his intention was certainly not to cast gloom and doom, it wasn't the most uplifting remark, especially to a group of aspiring

American capitalists.

Rather didn't elaborate on how, when, and why the U.S. would lose its standing — he quickly moved on to another topic. But there seems to be a number of factors — and combinations of them — that could do us in: our growing national debt, the economic and militaristic rise of other countries, environmental problems, rampant corruption, and of course, terrorism, along with the distractions caused by it. Whatever the case, history commands that something will eventually get you in the end, and maybe that was all Rather was implying. Maybe it was just his way of saying, "Enjoy it while you can."

Jeannie and I are still talking about the event — the people we saw, the elegance and majesty of the hotel, and, of course, what Dan Rather had to say. It's the kind of experience that grows on you over time, and you occasionally refer back to — even years later — at various gatherings of friends and family. "Remember when we saw Dan Rather?"

As much as I enjoyed the brush with celebrity, it was most refreshing to see Rather without the cameras, makeup, and script. Without all the elements of production, he even came across as being vulnerable. And though most of us never know exactly what happens to a news story as it makes its way through a television network's production team, we knew that on that particular night, we got an honest and thoughtful perspective on our world — and it was delivered by a man who has almost seen it all.

THE GARDEN SALAD ZONE

Appeared in Vegetarian Times *(January 2007)*

If you are a vegetarian who is vigilant about avoiding animal products, eating out can be a remarkably formidable experience. Short of going into the restaurant kitchen, interrogating the chef, and reading all the nutritional labels for the ingredients of your desired entrée, you must rely on your server for accurate information, honesty, and a reasonable command of the English language. Unfortunately, the combination of all three of these qualities is not all that common.

What's even more disconcerting is that many perfectly intelligent, English-speaking servers think that a tuna steak is vegetarian fare. It's as if they missed the animal-vegetable-mineral lesson in fifth grade. No Child Left Behind? We need a No Vegetable Left Behind program for our schools. Sometimes when I try to explain the concept of a vegetarian — or in my case, a vegan — wait staff look at me like I'm speaking in tongues.

The good news is that there are more and more restaurants that cater to herbivores, or at least accommodate us, with entrées like pasta primavera or veggie burgers. Asian establishments — Chinese, Indian, Thai, etc. — are often vegetarian-friendly, offering wonderfully flavorful dishes with meat substitutes such as tofu, wheat gluten, and legumes.

However, even those of us who have favorite vegetarian haunts will, at one time or another, end up dining at more traditional restaurants, such as Joe's Rib Shack, because we're on the road, or going to a place chosen by non-vegetarian friends, family members, or coworkers.

And it is these moments — when we vegetarians go head-to-head with the carnivorous world — that can be incredibly tense. Once you inform the server at Bill's Burger Hut that you don't eat meat, chicken, or fish, you have become the plant-based problem child. Out of your waiter's twenty current customers, you are the one person that won't eat 95 percent of the items on the menu. You have just entered the Garden Salad Zone.

The problem is: If you decide to leave the Garden Salad Zone, and go to the trouble to get the server to get the chef to concoct a vegetarian dish more interesting than a plate of lettuce and tomato, you may become the spectacle of your table and all the other guests around you. "Look honey, he doesn't eat meat. I wonder if he plays the tambourine, too."

Having lived in Iowa for three years — the nation's pork producing capital — I've eaten at many places that are the equivalent of Joe's Rib Shack, and sat next to friends and coworkers who devoured a massive slab of beef while I picked away at a salad. And I made it through those moments by ordering extra tomato and softly humming "Sound of Silence" to myself.

Though I believe it is important for vegetarians to be reasonably outspoken, I also believe there is a time and a place for doing so. Harry's House of Beef is not one of them.

However, make sure you do show your appreciation to servers who do go out of their way to meet your dining needs when you visit a more vegetarian-friendly restaurant. Tip well. Say thank you. Tell them how much you enjoyed the meal. Give them a hug. We vegetarians are known for our compassion and kindness — make sure you show it. Just leave your tambourine in the car.

ONCE UNBITTEN, TWICE SHY

I've been running for twenty years and logged more than 20,000 miles. Because I'm built like a fire plug — I have meaty legs and a sturdy lower torso — I've stayed free of most typical running injuries. I've had occasional mishaps: slipping on ice, tripping over curbs, and running into street signs and telephone poles at night. Fortunately, I've always picked myself up and kept going.

Like all veteran runners, I've encountered a plethora of dogs. Some just want to run with me, and I welcome them. It's a cheap ego boost when they run out of steam after just a few blocks. Then there are the sex fiends of the canine world who just want a whiff of my private parts, regardless of my gender or whether there's any mutual interest. Occasionally, I've come across the truly nasty dogs who are out for flesh. In all cases, my mantra has been to keep running and show no fear. That's worked without exception.

But then came my new next-door neighbor's dog. Let's just call him "Killer." I don't know his real name. He's about sixty pounds and looks like a cross between a terrier and a Doberman. Killer growls and barks incessantly at anything that comes near his front yard. My neighbor also has another dog — the nicest black Lab you'd ever want to meet. Let's just call him "Decoy."

Well, Killer and I developed an understanding right away. I never ran in front of his house and he left me alone. I always stayed across the street.

One recent morning, I stumbled out of bed to get in an early run.

I was still half asleep as I jogged past my front yard and approached Killer's house. I wasn't thinking about Killer at all. And because there are thick bushes that separate our yards, I didn't even see that he was outside. At first, he didn't see me either. There were no warning barks. All I remember was him coming at me like a heat-seeking missile, and me bolting in the opposite direction toward the street. Unfortunately, Killer's front yard is elevated about a foot-and-a-half off of the road. I went flying. The Wright Brothers would have been impressed with how long I stayed aloft.

The landing was ugly: two broken ribs, a deep bloody gash in my palm, and other assorted cuts and scrapes. Killer never touched me — he just stood there licking his chops as I peeled myself off of the pavement.

I called the police. When the two officers and I arrived at Killer's home, only Decoy was there in the front yard to greet us. For the record, Decoy loves people in uniform. He slobbered over the cops like nobody's business. Killer's owner was not stupid — he locked Killer up in the back bedroom.

Killer's owner told the cops and me that there was an electric fence and that Killer, "…just wanted you to pet him." Let me tell you, Killer wasn't thinking about affection — he wanted a dining experience.

I felt pathetic, because I never got bit. How would "almost bitten" sound in front of a judge? The police surely weren't going to back me up.

I eventually healed, but for two months, I experienced excruciating pain any time I laughed, sneezed, or made any sudden moves. My injuries, however, didn't stop me from running for very long; I was back on the road in less than a week, though I had to take it pretty slow for awhile to minimize the pain.

I'm running full-throttle again, but not without an acute fear of dog attacks. When I run, I feel like I'm a lone gazelle roaming the African plain destined to become some predator's next victim. I don't want to be the highlight of some nature channel episode.

I'm not one for carrying mace or a stick — I'm a vegetarian and don't want to hurt any animals. Some experts recommend that a person stop running if attacked by a dog. Rather, they should lay face down on the ground and remain motionless. I guess it's less sporting for a crazed canine to dismember a seemingly dead person.

As for Killer, he continues to harass passers-by. I hear him carrying on every day. But to my knowledge, he's never attacked anyone else. Maybe his owner has cranked up the power of his alleged electric fence. Maybe Killer has grown more accustomed to the pedestrian traffic in front of his house. Or maybe Killer's just waiting for me, the unclaimed prize that he never got to sink his teeth into — the runner with the meaty thighs.

MAKING NICE WITH VEGETARIANS — AN INSIDER'S GUIDE

Aired on WYPR, NPR in Baltimore (November 21, 2008)

There are about 25 million of us lurking in the United States. Actually, we don't lurk all that much. In fact, we can be a rather annoyingly outspoken, knowledgeable, and self-righteous bunch. We are the ones who kicked your ass in high school debate class, and continued to berate you with our arguments and opinions while you ran back to your locker. We are the vegetarians, and when it comes to espousing our opinions and beliefs, we take no prisoners. We are fundamentalists — instead of worshiping the Lord, we revere chickens, pigs, and cows. Many of us harbor small colonies of cats, dogs, and rabbits — a few dozen here, a few dozen there.

So, as a public service to the non-vegetarian majority, I feel compelled to offer some advice on how best to deal with and tolerate vegetarians. We really aren't all that bad, if you know our hot buttons: puppy mills, baby seal hunts, veal, and Jello, for example. (What — you didn't know that Jello is made from animal hooves? Don't let that dessert's seductive jiggle fool you.)

If you are already a vegetarian, give this article to your carnivorous friends and acquaintances. Consider it a goodwill gesture or a peace offering. It will help them understand you better. It will make them think you're acknowledging your difficult behavior, when in actuality, you're just feeding them more meat-free propaganda.

Resistance is futile

It really is silly to debate us about the health and environmental advantages of a vegetarian diet. The cards are overwhelmingly stacked against you. Most mainstream health organizations, including the American Dietetic Association, agree that a vegetarian diet will reduce your risk of cardiovascular disease, diabetes, certain cancers, and obesity. (Even if you're the type who thrives on junk food, you can still devour all the chips, Twinkies, and soda you want.)

Do you think you need meat to be a successful athlete? Well, track star Carl Lewis — Olympic Athlete of the Century and winner of nine gold medals — reached his performance peak as a vegan. Bill Pearl, a four-time Mister Universe, was at his best while on a vegetarian diet. (And yes, they are both still meat free.)

Do you think you need meat to be smart? Well, intellectual heavyweights by the names of Einstein and DaVinci seemed to get by OK on meat-free diets.

To me, the environmental debate for vegetarianism is even more of a slam dunk. Almost 80 percent of all agricultural land in the U.S. is used to raise animals for food or grow the grain that feeds them. What's even more stunning is the fact that farm animals produce about 130 times as much excrement as does the entire human population in the U.S. That's a lot of doo doo.

Know the lingo

You wouldn't think answering the question, "What is a vegetarian?" would be all that difficult. But it is, and unfortunately, it reveals that we vegetarians are not only ornery, we are complex and somewhat of a contradiction.

You can be considered a vegetarian even if you eat dairy and egg products. It's the dead animal products you need to avoid to officially be vegetarian. Herbivores of this ilk are known as lacto-ovo vegetarians. (Lacto for milk, ovo for egg.)

There are people out there who call themselves vegetarian even though they eat fish. Know that these fish-o-tarians irritate the hell out of the vegetarian purists. I'm not so dismissive. We need all the allies we can get, and at least they're confining their murderous ways to the seas. With them, you are still safe if you have legs.

Vegans are the real vegetarians, dismissing any products made from animals — dead or alive. Most Americans pronounce the word as: veegun. Vegans should not be confused with beings who come from somewhere near that bright star in the sky named Vega, nor should they be confused with a person who drove that crappy American car of the '70s known as a Vega. I am guessing that the guys who designed the Vega were a group of dyslexic, underachieving pot smokers. I never drove a Vega, but I did push one out of a ditch once. Those cars were the best thing to ever happen to the Japanese auto industry. And no, that quirky musician of the '90s Suzanne Vega is not a vegan.

Now if you really want to impress your animal-free friends, tell them that a Brit named Donald Watson came up with the word "vegan" by deleting the letters "etari" from "vegetarian." Thankfully, the chap lived to the ripe age of ninety-five. It would have been quite embarrassing for the veg movement if he had only made it to forty-three.

Tofu: get used to it

Tofu is important to vegetarians, because it is an excellent source of protein. Hang out with an herbivore long enough, and you will inevitably come face to face with tofu, be it soft, firm, fried, or baked.

Tofu is to a vegetarian like duct tape is to a handyman. You can do almost anything with tofu. But if you don't do anything to it, it in fact tastes like duct tape.

Though many people are mystified by tofu, it isn't all that mysterious. It is simply curdled soy milk, and made in much the same way cheese is made from cow's milk. I find it interesting how many people think tofu is revolting, yet they find cheese totally yummy. Frankly, I don't see what's so appetizing about eating food that ultimately came from the teat of a cow.

The secret to tasty tofu lies in the skill of the cook and the ingredients — the herbs, spices, and oils — used to supplement its flavorless disposition. My recommendation: Don't eat tofu dishes made by rookies. I've found that people botch tofu entrées at least a half-dozen times before they get it right. Some cooks never figure it out.

If you want to score points with your vegetarian friend, don't make faces when he or she talks about their favorite tofu dish. If you really want to bond with them, take them out to a restaurant that serves tofu dishes — they're often Asian establishments — and order a tofu entrée for yourself. Smile. Enjoy it. And don't forget to share.

Dining out with a vegetarian: welcome to my nightmare

There's nothing more daunting for an herbivore than eating out at a conventional restaurant, because so many wait staff don't have a clue about what a vegetarian does and doesn't eat. It's amazing how many servers think that anything but a steak will suffice. I wish I had a nickel for every time a waiter or waitress asked, "How about the chicken?" after I've informed them that I am vegetarian.

What's even more challenging for them is when I ask if a particular dish is flavored with chicken stock. It's a "deer-in-the-headlights" moment for many a server. It's as if you asked them to prove an advanced calculus theorem.

I often fantasize about a video game where the vegetarian player gets to disembowel and behead any wait staff who attempt to serve a non-vegetarian dish. You get bonus points for nabbing the waiter who tries to serve you the more inconspicuously non-veg entrée. (To keep it fair, you lose points if they attempt to serve an entrée that is in fact vegetarian.) They could call the game: Vegetarian Dining Massacre. Are you Xbox developers listening?

Anyway, the bottom line: If you go dining with a vegetarian, just be quiet and put up with our whining and server interrogations. The meal won't last forever, and the occasion will make a great story for the next day when you're eating hamburgers for lunch with your carnivorous coworkers.

Your final assignment

Speaking of hamburgers, here's a suggested evening of entertainment that will really help you connect with your vegetarian pals. Cozy up to the television with your friends, including your pets, and pop the PETA video "Meet Your Meat" in the DVD player. Unlike my video game fantasy, this is more what I call "reality TV." And we all know that reality TV is big these days.

After watching the video, maybe you'll be moved enough to

adopt a vegetarian lifestyle. Maybe not. But even if you don't decide to become an herbivore on the spot, you'll see that we, the meat-free, aren't completely wacko after all. We're just crazy about the animals.

MIAMI

I had high hopes for a better life when I moved from Washington, D.C., to Miami in 1998. After a decade of the high-tech rat race in the nation's capital, I was ready for something meaningful. The offer to work as a hospice-care writer was quite alluring. I imagined I'd be recording the dramatic confessions of the dying, stuff like "I rigged the Bingo operation on Biscayne Boulevard" or "I was the Hialeah flasher." Women would be drawn to my altruistic, Gandhi-like persona, offering up their firm, bronzed bodies.

What I got was a desk job writing white papers about morphine titration and physician-assisted suicide. I quickly learned that beautiful women with tight bodies and tans wanted beautiful men with tight bodies and tans. I was a short, Jewish vegetarian whose eczema went haywire in South Florida's oppressive heat and humidity. The only thing I did get was a catcall from a drunken transvestite on South Beach...or maybe he stepped on a piece of glass.

Miami is great if you are gay, retired or Latino. Even if I decided to succumb to my Jewish heritage and join a temple, I couldn't handle tanned rabbis with white shoes. That's just wrong.

The trauma of my move to the Sunshine State began as soon as I took possession of my apartment. Two days after I moved in, I had to evacuate because Hurricane Georges was bearing down on South Florida, and I happened to pick a place right on Biscayne Bay. Through friends back in D.C., I was able to contact some locals, Sue and Michelle, who invited me to stay in their pastor's inland home. My newfound friends were with a Presbyterian church, and all they asked was that I help put up some storm shutters for members of their congregation. Best of all, they didn't try to convert me, and they had satellite TV — 500 stations!

Just before I evacuated, while on a street-corner pay phone in Miami Beach desperately trying to get renter's insurance, I was approached by three young Orthodox Jewish men, dressed in black, carrying prayer books and a Shofar (ceremonial horn). They asked me to join them for an impromptu celebration of the Jewish New Year. Were these proselytizing Jews divine intervention or a bizarre scheme that my mother dreamt up?

Given the fact that I was on hold and in need of good karma (you need good karma if you are going to get insurance when a hurricane is approaching), I agreed to participate in their Rosh Hashanah Road Show. As I waited on the phone, they recited a couple prayers, sounded the Shofar, wished me good luck and scooted down the street in search of their next gig. A few minutes later, I got an insurance policy and headed out to my Presbyterian refuge. I was feeling good — I was now covered by Nationwide and the New and Old Testaments. As fate would have it, Georges missed the Florida mainland completely.

Over the next few months, I spent my time learning Spanish, writing anti-Kervorkian propaganda, and discovering new ways to scratch my eczema. Also, call me misinformed, but for Halloween, I managed to be the only straight male in South Florida to dress up as Dorothy from The Wizard of Oz.

When New Years rolled around, I was definitely ready for "out with the old." I received a party invitation from my friends Sue and Michelle — they were going to have a small informal gathering at their place.

After a pleasant meal and after-dinner chat, Michelle began talking about a comedic writer named David Sedaris. I had never heard of him. And though I enjoy good humor, her obsession with this guy seemed a bit odd. She went on and on. "You have to get his book *Holidays on Ice*…Have you heard him on NPR?…Oh, I just love him!" Finally, at about 11:30 p.m., she strong-armed us on to the outdoor patio to hear a reading of Sedaris' *SantaLand Diaries*. (It was either that or the fiftieth installment of "Dick Clark's New Year's Rockin' Eve.")

As we cleaned off patio furniture and lit citronella candles to fend off the bugs, I noticed that it sounded like the Fourth of July outside. Booms and bangs came from both far and near — some sounded uncomfortably loud and close. I was casually informed that on New Year's Eve, it is a tradition for Miamians to shoot off their guns. "Don't worry," Sue said, "They are shooting them in the air." "Where do bullets land?" I asked the group. "Are falling bullets dangerous?" My questions were answered with quizzical looks and shoulder shrugs. The one thing I concluded was that the NRA should be doing very well in this neck of the woods.

So, with random gunfire in the background and flashlight in hand, Michelle read through SantaLand Diaries gleefully, as we all giggled, snorted, and roared through Sedaris' classic hard-luck story of how his dream of becoming a television writer turned into pathetic, humiliating work as an elf — complete with green tights, vomiting children and sadistic Santas — at Macy's in New York City.

I am happy to report that I survived the falling bullets and Sedaris reading of New Year's Eve 1999. And, I moved from Miami four months later. The fact that I ended up in the middle of Iowa just a short time afterward is another story, which conveniently appears next.

IOWA

On a Friday afternoon in June 2000, I departed Reagan National, an airport abuzz with sweaty Type A's rushing to their gates, pulling carry-ons, lugging laptops, and clutching cell phones and double lattes. A few hours later, I disembarked into the vacuous concourse at Des Moines "International" Airport. A lone cleaning person wandered aimlessly, unable to locate anything to sweep into his bin.

Outside the terminal, there was no taxi line or policemen directing traffic. The parking lot was empty beyond the second row. This was like an *Outer Limits* episode where an entire population had disappeared without explanation.

In my top ten reasons to avoid Internet dating, number one is: dismemberment by chainsaw. Number two is: abduction by satanic cults. Number three is: falling in love and moving to Iowa, but it's climbing the chart with a bullet.

Even Iowans, when they learned I moved from D.C., ask, "Why the *hell* did you move *here*? To which I answered with a shoulder shrug, mumbling and then an uncontrollable fit of coughing.

I moved from our nation's capital to our nation's corn capital under this spell for a soon-to-be divorcée named Melanie. Unlike Kincaid, the gallivanting photographer in the novel, *Bridges of Madison County*, I wasn't passing through Iowa for a quickie. I was coming for the long haul.

It didn't take me long to figure out that Iowa is one massive cornfield dotted with churches, Wal-Marts, oversized mutant pick-up trucks, and during the fall, rabid packs of college football fans (i.e., satanic cults). *The Washington Post* makes *The Des Moines Register* look like a placemat.

There were some positives to living there: Anorexia is virtually non-existent. English has been declared the state's official language. There's no traffic; it's easy to get where you're going, if you consider the *History of the Prairie* exhibit going somewhere. And, the mayor of Des Moines hasn't been videotaped smoking crack-cocaine in a local hotel.

Also, if you like fairs, Iowa's is world-renowned. It's the indisputable highlight of the year here. You can ponder spectacles such as the "Butter Cow," a life-sized sculpture of a cow made of butter. Bring lots of toast.

Unfortunately, as a vegetarian, I had a problem with the fair's massive showing of soon-to-be-slaughtered livestock. I felt like I was going to Porky Pig's Last Supper, and HE is the last supper. (When he stutters, "That's all folks," he's not kidding.)

The indisputable low point of the year in Iowa was that first winter, which ran from September through June. It was brutal even by Iowa standards. Snowfall and temperature records were shattered. Though I was hoping to build my freelance writing career, I spent more time in freelance snow removal, and adding extra columns and rows to my wind-chill temperature chart. Winter in Iowa is like the *Outer Limits* episode where the earth moves slightly out of orbit from the sun, and suddenly enters another Ice Age.

My relationship with the now-divorced, Web-surfing farm girl ended after only a year. But with a new job, I decided to make a go of it in corn country, at least for a little while.

To keep my spirits up, I tried to maintain the *Outer Limits* metaphor; I viewed it like a trip to another planet. I came sardonically, but peacefully. I took a few soil samples, milked some cows and enjoyed some fried Twinkies at the State Fair. If you happened to hear about crop circles in Iowa in late 2003, don't worry. It was just me marking a landing site for the return of my mother ship.

FORTY-SIX YEARS, FORTY-SEVEN QUESTIONS

Appeared in Opium Magazine *(online, November 2007)*

1961: Who turned the lights on? **1962:** Why do I make poopie?
1963: Why can't I play on the stove? **1964:** What's under this lady's
dress? **1965:** Why do girls have cracks instead of pee pees? **1966:**
Why doesn't GI Joe have a pee pee? **1967:** When can I become
a professional wrestler? **1968:** Why do hippies smell funny? **1969:**
What's a nigger? **1970:** Why does our rabbi have hair growing out
of his nose? **1971:** What will happen if we blow off an entire pack of
firecrackers in this box of Rice Crispies? **1972:** When will I get hair
on my balls? **1973:** Why are the pages of this *Playboy* magazine
stuck together? **1974:** Will I ever kiss a girl? **1975:** Will I ever get
laid? **1976:** Sensimilla or Columbian? **1977:** Want to camp out at
the stadium before the Pink Floyd concert? **1978:** Do you think
Howard has gotten laid yet? **1979:** Should I use a rubber? **1980:**
Do you want to live together? **1981:** Pizza again? **1982:** Should I
cut my hair? **1983:** Why do we have to get married? **1984:** Why do
you have to leave me? **1985:** Which psychotherapists are covered
under my insurance plan? **1986:** Want to come back to my place and
see my collection of rare etchings? **1987:** Haven't we met before?
1988: Want to come back to my place and see my collection of
rare Albanian sculptures? **1989:** Will you marry me? **1990:** Will you
get out of my life? **1991:** Can I get that burger without meat? **1992:**
Will you take my TV? **1993:** Why isn't my psychotherapy covered
under my insurance plan? **1994:** Who's in the white Bronco? **1995:**
Were you the master of your domain? **1996:** Why is the CEO of my

company earning more money than all of Zambia? **1997:** Can I get that Frappuccino with extra mocha? **1998:** Why did I move to Miami? **1999:** Will I ever get laid again? **2000:** Does Al Gore have a pulse? **2001:** Does George Bush have a clue? **2002:** Peace or oil? **2003:** Why did I move to Des Moines? **2004:** Want to see my Web site? **2005:** Agnostic or atheist? **2006:** Nano or Shuffle? **2007:** How far does that colonoscope go?

SAVE ME, VEGANS!

Aired on WYPR, NPR in Baltimore (September 19, 2008)

In July 2008, my girlfriend, Jeannie, and I ventured to a local park to take some photos for the cover of *The Vegan Monologues*. Frankly, I had been struggling with concepts for the cover for many weeks. I had recruited various graphically talented friends and acquaintances to come up with prototypes, but none of their efforts clicked with me. My latest idea was a shot of me with some aesthetic or ironic arrangement of carrots.

When I first came up with the concept, it seemed very cool to me, but as I drove to the park hauling a camera, my girlfriend, and bunches of carrots, the whole thing began to feel very silly. So I was testy, and my girlfriend – let's just say she's no Annie Leibovitz – was not thrilled with the photo assignment either.

Things went from not-so-good to worse as the wind picked up and the sky clouded over. It was already an uncomfortably sticky day. We finally picked a spot for our shoot next to a wooded area. I began to perspire and mutter expletives as I stuck carrots in my pants pockets for the first shots. A woman looking on instructed her kids to "stay with mommy."

As I was waiting for Jeannie to find the shutter button on the camera, I heard the high-pitched cries of a cat emerging from the woods. He headed straight for us.

Though the sound coming from the cat sounded like "Meow! Meow! Meow! Meow!" it could be easily translated into English as "Save me, save me, vegans!"

That was the end of photo shoot. The second coming of Jesus was not going to stop Jeannie from rescuing this cat. In fact, for Jeannie, a stray animal is the second coming of Jesus.

This poor cat was wet, dirty, and in dire need of a square meal. He clearly was not feral and hadn't been fairing well in the wilds of Roland Park. While I was worried that he was going to give us fleas and the bubonic plague, Jeannie was giving this cat as much love and attention as any mother would give her sick child.

We quickly got the cat over to the vet, who determined that all he needed was to be de-wormed, bathed, and fed. The next evening, we brought him home to Jeannie's. We named him Woody because he came from the woods. Jeannie's other cat, Chester, was not exactly thrilled to have another cat arrive on the scene. Chester liked being king.

There was some tension and hissing between Chester and Woody, but over time, they started getting used to each other. It's funny how humans are usually polite and friendly when they first meet. It's the long-term relationships that are often more challenging. But cats are pretty upfront with their anxieties, and with a little luck, they work it out and get along with each other for life.

Though many of we vegans are food aficionados, it's the animals – especially those strays like Woody – that touch our heart strings and put us on the meat-free path. Sure there are animal lovers who aren't vegan and vegans who aren't crazy about animals. But for so many of us, compassion for animals is an incredibly humanizing force. Actually, I would argue that most people are vegan to some extent – just some of us are more so than others.

I have to say, it's quite coincidental that Woody entered our lives while we were working on a vegan book project. But then again, maybe he was waiting for the right people to come along before he made his plea for rescue. With a little strategic timing on his part, a few cries of "Save me, vegans!" was all it took.

VEGETARIAN GUYS GET THE GIRLS

I've been to more vegetarian gatherings than any avid herbivore could ever dream of — countless potlucks, parties, protests, fairs, and fundraisers. Through them all, two things have held constant: an absence of meat and an abundance of women.

When I became a vegetarian, I did it for the animals — not to meet girls. But alas, there they were. Women came by the busloads to vegetarian events, and nobody was selling Tupperware or lingerie.

Remember those Elvis movies where all these voluptuous women would gather around him when he arrived at a party? Nothing remotely similar to that has ever happened to me at a veg event, but I have had a couple of remarkably stimulating conversations about tofu with the opposite sex.

I am not currently in the market for a woman — a disclaimer I make to ensure continued harmony with my extraordinarily lovely and multitalented vegan girlfriend, Jeannie. But for the guys who are looking to start a relationship, going vegetarian is a great way to meet women and lots of them.

My friend Don "Dapper Don" Robertson runs the Baltimore chapter of Earthsave — a global organization promoting a plant-based lifestyle — and he draws from 50 to 100 people to his monthly speaking events and potlucks. Don reports that on average, about 65 percent of attendees are women. That's two females for every male. Not too shabby.

What's also not too shabby about the vegetarian lifestyle for guys is that it makes us better lovers. Don't get me wrong. I am not saying that all vegetarian guys are well-oiled sex machines, but a meat-free diet will keep your arteries clear including those that power the family jewels. Medical studies have shown that atherosclerosis can lead to impotence.

If you are concerned that going vegetarian is going to negatively impact your bodybuilding and toning efforts at the gym, worry not man of steel. There are plenty of professional he-men who have done quite well on meat-free diets including four-time Mister Universe Bill Pearl.

If you prefer athletic endeavors that require endurance or speed, you can look to vegan Carl Lewis — winner of nine Olympic track and field gold medals — for inspiration to give up meat.

But even if you are not the type to woo women with your athletic prowess or flawless physique, the fact that you're vegetarian says something important about your personality and your values. As an herbivore, there's a good chance you have compassion for animals and the environment. Maybe you'll even talk about your feelings and hold your partner's purse when she goes to the ladies' room. (Hopefully it is a small purse you can discreetly tuck under your arm.) These are the habits and character traits that vegetarian women just adore. Even non-vegetarian women dig those qualities.

The only downside to being a vegetarian guy is that once you have met the woman of your dreams, she'll probably end up taking you to even more vegetarian gatherings than you went to before you met her. Hopefully, there will be another guy or two you can hang out with and talk to about your favorite baseball team or Pink Floyd concert. And if you really hit it off, maybe you'll even exchange tofu recipes.

THREE DAYS IN OKLAHOMA

Appeared in The Oklahoman *(March 31, 2007)*

When I strolled into Oklahoma City for the Will Rogers Writing Conference, I wasn't sure what to expect. As a vegetarian urbanite from Baltimore, Oklahoma City wasn't exactly on my must-see list. All I knew was that the area was flat and the setting for a remarkably popular Broadway musical.

Even though I was holed up in the convention center for much of the weekend, I was able to experience a number of attractions and much of the community's culture. I met a few cowboys, a couple of Cherokees, and even heard Will Rogers' grandson Kem give a short speech. While out jogging down Robinson Avenue on St. Patrick's Day, I was joined for a couple of blocks by a few festive young men clad in green dresses. They were friendly, but notably disappointed I was not wearing green clothing to commemorate the holiday.

My visit one evening to the National Cowboy Museum was a wonderful treat. I'll never forget seeing the mammoth James Fraser sculpture — I call it *Tired Indian* — that greets you when you enter the building. After a long day of lectures and workshops, I would have made a good model for a piece called *Tired Writer*.

The Oklahoma City National Museum was an incredibly moving experience for me — especially on a cold and windy night with a train roaring in the distance. While you're there, you can't help but wonder about those tragic moments in April 1995, and what the victims' family and friends must still be going through today. You think about your own loved ones, and how much their happiness and safety means to you.

Conference attendees and I also got the opportunity to attend a reception at *The Oklahoman* newspaper headquarters. Among the festivities, we heard Editor Ed Kelley tell a great story about a sports writer's encounter with a tornado — a tale that was uniquely Oklahoman.

But what impressed me most about Oklahoma was the conference namesake, Will Rogers. I felt ambivalent about him at first. Though his many pursuits were impressive — his roping, acting, and writing — I couldn't understand why he was so popular. He wasn't a polished literary craftsman, and when he spoke, he often lacked grammatical accuracy. His tilted hat made him look goofy and uneducated. These were my first impressions of a man I had previously known little about.

After returning to Baltimore, I had some time to process what I learned about Will Rogers. I wondered what Will would think if he were alive today. How would he fit in our society? Would he be an Internet junkie, e-mailing and blogging his observations and opinions until the wee hours of the morning? Would he be appalled by the crime and drug problems that plague cities such as Baltimore? Would he think that vegetarians like me are extreme, or would he himself be a vegetarian, because of the benefits to one's health and the environment? What would he think of the wars we perpetuate on the other side of the world? Obviously, we'll never know the answers to these questions, and how he would have faired in today's world.

But when I consider the public voices and figures that inspire me now as a writer — people such as Garrison Keillor, Dan Rather, George Carlin, and David Letterman — I see Will Rogers' wit and sensibility in each and everyone of them. It's hard to think of a respected journalist, commentator, or comedian who doesn't incorporate something from Rogers' character. In that sense, he is one of the most pervasive figures in America today.

I may never come back to Oklahoma, but the impressions I took away with me during my three-day trip will be long lasting — the people, the landmarks, the stories, and the beautiful, wide-open terrain. And though I learned a lot about the life and times of Will Rogers during my visit, what was most enlightening was the realization that he made his mark on me long before I ever set foot in the state.

HOW WE SAID GOODBYE

Jeannie and I recently euthanized her nineteen-year-old cat, Delilah. As so many of us know, it's a heartbreaking task.

Delilah was a beautiful girl with thick black fur and a white stomach and paws. Her green eyes were confident and at times even authoritative. Delilah knew she was pretty, and used her good looks to persuade us to do just about anything she wanted. She would howl when she wanted us to join her upstairs, demand food when she was hungry, and reprimand us when we had been away from home for more than a couple of hours. Then there were the times when she sprawled out on her favorite piece of carpet, waiting for me to lull her into complete contentment with petting and scratching.

But kidney disease and just plain old age brought her to the point where everyday living was a struggle. There were moments toward the end when Delilah would relax on the front lawn or nose around the garden after dark. Her eyes might even catch the movement of a low-flying bird. But physically, she had wasted away to a creature that was of little resemblance to the plump, spry queen of a cat she had once been.

We went through a similar process with Delilah's brother, Samson, more than two years ago. The fact that a drug addict had temporarily owned the brother and sister cats when they were kittens, and unwittingly named them after Biblical lovers, is a little awkward and even mildly amusing, but ultimately, inconsequential. They were wonderful companions for Jeannie, and great friends to me in their later years. Having come into their world late in their lives, I was affectionately known as step daddy — a moniker I was proud of, especially never having had a child, or a pet of my own since I was a kid.

Letting go of these lovely and loving creatures is painful; it's one of the most difficult things we humans do. It seems cruel and unfair that they are taken from us. They don't want or require much — even the more demanding ones like Delilah don't ask for a lot — and they become our best friends. Unlike we humans who need to own, conquer, and accomplish things, cats and dogs are Zen-like in their approach to living. And we delight in that fact; just a treat or scratch on the head and they are content.

During the days before Delilah was put down, the three of us spent many hours on the porch just watching and listening to the world around us. They were perfect summer days — sunny, not too warm, and breezy. Those are the best memories. Just the three of us hanging out, enjoying the moment.

During those final hours, I wondered a lot about where Delilah would go after she passed. What would be her fate — what is our fate — beyond this life as we know it? All I could hope for was that Delilah was going to a good place. Maybe a place with Samson and her other siblings. Maybe a place with the same affection we had given her. Maybe a place where she could relax and just take in a summer day as we did so many times. Or maybe a place that is beyond our comprehension, but a good and loving place nonetheless. I had little choice but to let go of my friend, and hope that she would be well.

For those of us like Jeannie and me who don't profess an organized religion or afterlife, we go with what we have and that's mostly memories. We aren't much for ceremony or formality. After the vet came by the house and put Delilah down, her body ended up in the fridge vegetable cooler by the end of the evening. Then there was the trip the next day to the budget crematorium — with unkempt weed-ridden landscaping that Hitchcock would have relished — to drop off the body. And then a trip back the following day to get the ashes with Jeannie continually asking, "How do we know they're *her* ashes?" I responded pithily, "We don't. How about Chinese for lunch?"

Throughout the process, we don't pray, per se; we just hope. We cry a lot and then we keep going. There's no church, synagogue, or mosque. There's no known afterlife — just the unknown after.

I do glean some hope when I hear the leaves rustling in the wind or watch an enormous flock of birds roost in the tall tree. I find salvation in the way the world just keeps moving forward. Nature has a way of settling me down.

I might put on a song by Harold Arlen or Leonard Bernstein to cheer me up. They are two guys who put together wonderful dreams of something good around the bend — somewhere over the rainbow; somewhere there's a place for us.

Ultimately, though, it just takes a lot of time to work through the pain and grief. For me, there will never be another Samson and Delilah. All I can do now is think of them fondly and often. And I wonder: Maybe sometimes they find their way back to us in the warm summer wind. Regardless, I'll be on the porch waiting for them.

PART TWO

TWIGS AND SEEDS

THE OTHER ESSAYS

HARDCORE ENTOMOLOGY

Appeared in Clean Sheets Magazine *(online, May 10, 2006)*

While driving down the freeway recently, I noticed a big greenish-yellowish blob on my right windshield wiper. Upon further inspection, I realized it was two grasshoppers mating, doggy-style. Because grasshoppers came — evolutionarily speaking — before canines, it might be more fitting to call their mating position "grasshopper-style."

In case you are wondering how I knew that the grasshoppers were actually mating rather than just embracing, I did a little research on the Internet. It's incredible how much insect porn is out there: photos, diagrams, and graphic descriptions. One innocent-enough-looking Web page from the University of Wyoming reports, "...a male usually approaches a female stealthily and pounces on her...invariably mounts the female from behind, lowers the tip of his abdomen below hers and attaches the genitalia." Whew, this is not the Styrofoam and straight-pin stuff from my eighth-grade biology class.

Anyway, I was amazed by the fact that these two grasshoppers could hang on to one another, and the oh-so erotic windshield wiper of my '89 Volvo, as I was doing sixty miles an hour down the highway. I could even see their little antennae fluttering in the wind.

Was this fast-moving fornication exciting for these insects? Or did the male climax prematurely from the anxiety of being on a speeding car? Does the female even care? Maybe she likes her sex quick. "Three seconds! Honey, you're the best!"

Something tells me that this couple did not have an extended courtship: No wining and dining, no foreplay, no "let's cuddle for a few hours after we're done." No, the male just pulled down his little grasshopper pants, the female said, "Wow," and away they went.

Clearly, they have few inhibitions, and it looks as though they may be into public displays of affection. Given the dangerous nature of this mating venue, one could easily argue that they're masochistic, as well. Maybe they're swingers, hopping — so to speak — from one partner to another.

Regardless, for me, their reckless abandon was liberating. With violence, adultery, sexually transmitted diseases, birth control and gender identification complicating the sexual practices of we humans, I found it refreshing to see two creatures just going at it.

Unfortunately, though, this story did not have a happy ending. About a mile from my exit, they couldn't hold onto my car any longer and were whisked away into dense midday traffic.

I do take consolation in knowing that despite their untimely demise, at least they went to the great grasshopper hereafter with grinning mandibles.

MY BEAUTY AND HER BEAST

Appeared in the Chicago Tribune *(August 25, 2005)*

My head hangs low as I head up the front walk of my girlfriend Jeannie's house on a Saturday afternoon. I'm humming that slow, familiar Bob Dylan dirge: "Ooooooo, ooooooo, ooo-ooo-ooo-ooo, knock, knock, knockin' on heaven's door."

Are we breaking up? No. Did someone die? No. Are we going shopping for a new designer toilet-bowl brush? No, but maybe later. The reason for my somber mood? I'm about to mow Jeannie's lawn.

It's not really a lawn — it's more like a half-acre, knee-high garden of sadism. Occasional blades of grass cower under the shadow of flesh-eating weeds. The pulsating, high-pitched buzz emanating from the back yard is not from crickets, but rather a sophisticated communications system inherent to alien plant forms. As I approach the lawn with a push mower circa the Eisenhower administration, the buzz turns into more of a belly laugh. "It's only grass," I keep saying to myself, over and over. "It's only grass."

Because I've lived in apartments my entire life, I never had to mow any lawns. That is, until Jeannie and her yard from hell entered my life. And because she prefers to do things naturally and organically—no chemicals or pesticides—I'm in a position of total weakness. With so little ammunition at my disposal, I might as well be Gandhi and try to talk the lawn into submission. I can imagine myself saying something like, "Let us agree on a mutually harmonious growth level," as a vine wraps around my ankle and drags me into the bushes.

But I quickly learned that the best approach to cutting "The Beast" was to take on each patch of growth relentlessly and just hack away, letting the blades of the ancient push mower chew away. Sometimes, I attack a section on two fronts: I go at it from one direction and then go over it again from a different angle. Other times, a running start works well, especially if the growth is particularly thick. It's ugly, demoralizing and very hard on the arms. But good old brute force is the way I get the job done. Do I bag the clippings, trim the edges and leave pretty symmetrical rows? Did Genghis Khan send out condolence cards?

The real victory for me came midway through the summer when I got the weed whacker working. I want to hug the dude who invented that ingenious device. There's nothing more exhilarating than ripping through stubborn plants with that baby in your hands. I instantly turn anything left behind by the lawn mower into toast.

I used to envy people who cut their lawns with riding tractors. But now, those wimps look to me like they're on kiddie rides at an amusement park. I can't even bear to watch employees of landscape companies in action with their big, shiny trucks and matching T-shirts. They're not cutting grass, they're having a tailgate party.

As the summer comes to a close, I'm getting accustomed to the weekly offenses on Jeannie's lawn. I'm beginning to appreciate some of the plants and foliage: the wild blackberries; the young evergreen and cedar trees; the butterfly and mulberry bushes. I enjoy watching the neighborhood birds devour the seed in the back-yard feeder and take refreshing breaks in the birdbath. Occasionally, I see a squirrel or rabbit darting across the yard. It makes me want to invite Wilford Brimley over for a bowl of Grape-Nuts.

Don't get me wrong. I'll welcome the winter respite from landscaping. Sure there may be snow to shovel or ice to chip, but it won't be anything like the weekly battles with "The Beast" under the oppressive summer sun. In preparation for next spring, maybe I'll polish and oil Jeannie's push mower, tighten its bolts and sharpen its blades. Maybe I'll get a new spool of monofilament for the weed whacker and recharge its battery. For me, some calisthenics are definitely in order: push-ups, sit-ups, jumping jacks, even a little kick-boxing. I'm going to be in tip-top shape. In April, when the lawn threatens to overtake us again, I'll be ready. "The Beast" will be begging for mercy. I assure you, after the mowing is done, you'll see nothing but clippings blowin' in the wind and me with Jeannie at the mall in search of that coveted toilet-bowl brush.

SLOW LEARNER NOW GETS BEING JEWISH

Appeared in the Chicago Tribune *(March 30, 2007)*

On Labor Day in 1969, at the age of eight, I broke into Taylor Road Elementary School in Cleveland Heights, Ohio, with six other kids and vandalized the school's library, restrooms and teachers lounges. The opening of school was delayed for three days because we did such a good job of tearing the place apart.

Ironically, the chief mastermind of the destruction, an older boy and well-established neighborhood troublemaker, lived across the street from Taylor, and his mother called the police when she spotted some kids hanging out of the school's windows. Without realizing it, she busted her own son along with the rest of us.

As the youngest and smallest of the proclaimed juvenile delinquents — and the only one who bawled hysterically throughout the court hearing — the judge went easy on me. I got off with trespassing, probation and a $25 fine.

However, my divorced parents, in a rare collaborative moment, were not so lenient. They sentenced me to Hebrew school. What better way to keep little Benny off the streets and get him in touch with his Jewish heritage?

And so began what was supposed to be my path to Judaic enlightenment.

For the next three years, I attended afternoon Hebrew school four days a week. While most of my friends, even the Jewish ones, were playing baseball, going to the candy store or watching *The Three Stooges* on TV when they got home from school, I was getting on a bus to go learn a language that moves across the page in the wrong direction and uses vowels optionally.

Why couldn't I have been just a neglected latch-key kid?

At my Hebrew school, there was no show and tell, no games, no movies — just the rote memorization of the Hebrew language and Torah study. We also learned about the ancient characters in Jewish history: Abraham, Isaac, Judah and the Maccabees, King Solomon and Queen Esther. And though the Three Stooges were all Jewish, they unfortunately weren't part of our stimulating curriculum.

Neither of my parents ever did much to reinforce our Jewish heritage at home, though my family did celebrate Passover. The highlight of our Passovers was the ceremonial meal called the seder. For many hours, my family would discuss and taste each symbolic, mouthwatering item on the seder plate, which included parsley, horseradish, a bone and a boiled egg. With a few strips of bacon, the seder plate would have made the perfect meal for the Atkins diet.

During our seders, there also was discussion of the ten plagues believed to be a punishment from God that befell the Egyptians for their enslavement of the Jewish people. These plagues ranged from frogs to boils to slaying of the firstborn. My innovative family developed its own plague for the seder: chain-smoking. We took the "slaying of the firstborn" concept to a new level: "Slaying of anyone breathing."

My relatives spent the rest of the evening kibitzing — mostly complaining about the hippies and President Nixon. "They're all meshugeh," my grandfather would groan as he tapped his cigarette on the side of an overflowing ashtray.

The final stage of my formal Jewish education took place in beautiful Pompano Beach, Florida. I moved there in 1972. Though there was a local synagogue, there was no Hebrew school, per se

— only Sunday school. So my sentence was immediately cut by 75 percent — just one day a week instead of four!

My parents' plan at that point was to get me to learn just enough Torah so I could have a bar mitzvah and officially become a Jewish man. I had a different plan.

As they say in real estate, it comes down to location, location, location. Our apartment complex in Pompano happened to be just a few blocks away from a canal teeming with fish. And our unit happened to be next to the home of Rick, a nice gentile boy who loved to fish as much as I did.

After my many months of Sunday morning angling expeditions with Rick, my mother was notified that I rarely showed up for class. At that point, she and my dad threw in the towel — they gave up on the bar mitzvah plan. I was freed from bondage! It was like my own personal Passover.

For the next thirty-plus years, I never looked back. I occasionally got dragged to synagogue by a girlfriend, but the operative word there is dragged. I even played in a Jewish softball league for a few years, but the operative word there is softball.

However, a recent chance encounter with a charming woman named Bluma Shapiro gave me a new perspective on being Jewish. I never actually met Bluma; I only heard her briefly on a radio program during my lunch hour.

Bluma described her miraculous story of survival during the Holocaust. She talked about how the Nazis occupied her hometown of Bialystok, Poland; how she unsuccessfully tried to hide from them in an underground system of bunkers; how she regularly saw Jews shot at point-blank range for the most arbitrary reasons; how she ended up being a prisoner in five concentration camps, including the infamous Auschwitz; and how after liberation, she returned to

Bialystok to learn that every single member of her immediate family had been killed.

While I was listening to Bluma, it occurred to me for the first time that the Holocaust was never discussed during my Hebrew school career. For that matter, no one in my immediate family — parents, grandparents, aunts, uncles — ever talked about it either. Did they think the story was too shocking for a growing boy — at a time when that boy was watching graphic footage of the Vietnam War and civil rights movement every day on prime-time television?

It also occurred to me that the Holocaust ended just sixteen years before I was born. When I was a kid, sixteen years seemed like an eternity. World War II was ancient history to me. But now, at forty-six, it gives me chills to think that the Holocaust ended just sixteen years before my arrival on this planet.

I was incredulous to realize that my Jewish elders chose not to educate me about a period in our history that was so incredibly horrifying on such a grand scale. Furthermore, unlike those familiar stories from the Old Testament — those greatest hits from Hebrew school — the Holocaust is very recent history. There are even eyewitnesses like Bluma Shapiro still alive to tell the gruesome tale. Bluma is in her mid-eighties, but still spends a lot of time talking to school groups about her experiences.

"Though it takes a lot out of me, I believe the reason for my survival is I have to talk about it," she says. "People say it didn't happen. I lost my whole family — my parents, five siblings, aunts, uncles. No one survived. This is why I have to talk about it — no matter how much it costs me emotionally and psychologically."

Despite my parents' best intentions, I never developed much of an appreciation for my Jewish heritage. I doubt I'll ever have the urge to attend Sabbath services, buy a yarmulke or lead a Passover seder. I have no regrets about balking at that sacred rite of passage, the bar mitzvah.

But thanks to Bluma Shapiro's remarkable story of survival and courage, and her tireless conviction to keep on telling it, I am beginning to understand what it means to be a Jewish man.

THE FURTHER ADVENTURES OF ECZEMA BOY

Updated from an earlier version of this article, which appeared in
The Washington Post *(July 11, 2000)*

When my allergist declared that I had the worst case of adult eczema that he has ever seen, I was stunned. And impressed. "Wow," I thought to myself. "A lifetime achievement award for bad skin!" But who do I thank, the Academy of Skin Disease Arts and Sciences? And how about all the little people who make eczema possible?

Not that my achievements have ever gone unnoticed. When I have an outbreak of the red, crusty and swollen eruptions — which is to say, nearly all the time — everyone knows it. Whether I am at work, on a date, at the grocery store or just looking at myself in the mirror while brushing my teeth, there it is, rampant on my face, around my eyes and covering much of the rest of my body. My forehead is particularly bad. There I get dry, red, crusty patches. When it gets really bad, it erupts into scabs.

I get questions and stares on a regular basis. Kids are especially awed. When kids stare at me, I want to say, "No, I'm not the Creature from the Black Lagoon, but I did meet him once at an autograph signing." Or, puffing out my chest and striking a suitably heroic cartoon pose: "Not to fear, young man, I am Eczema Boy, and I defeat evildoers by hypnotizing them with my incessant scratching and picking! Step back, there's some radioactive ooze now!" But, of course, I don't. I just pretend I don't see them staring.

Many of the people I know — co-workers, family, friends — often ask how my skin is. And, like most how-are-you niceties, it's really a rhetorical question. If they know me at all, they know that the last time I could honestly answer that question with "pretty good," Gerald Ford was singing the praises of Whip Inflation Now.

What was so difficult about hearing my doctor's comment about reaching the dermatologic pinnacle was that I had been quite aggressive about treating my condition. This was not like the guy who never mows his lawn getting the Ugly Yard award. This was like the guy who busts butt every weekend with his weed whacker and fertilizer winning the dubious distinction.

I share my affliction with about fifteen million Americans. Also known as atopic dermatitis, eczema is a chronic, hereditary disease that is allergy-related. Anything from food to dust mites to extremes in weather may trigger an outbreak.

Because by all appearances I am allergic to every element in the periodic table, it is impossible for me to avoid the stuff that causes it. Though eczema is common in babies and children, they often grow out of it. As I have gotten older, I have somehow managed to grow into it, with the condition getting considerably worse over time.

Though there is no cure for eczema, there are a number of simple, conventional treatments that provide relief for people with milder cases. These treatments don't faze my condition, however. They only make it laugh.

For instance, many people use hypoallergenic moisturizers to relieve the dryness; hard cases may prefer petroleum jelly, which seals in moisture rather than just applying it from the outside. Over-the-counter cortisone creams and ointments can significantly and safely — if briefly — reduce itching, swelling and redness. (I use them regularly, and get only minor relief.) Antihistamines, over-the-counter and prescription, are also used to relieve itching.

Some people get relief through sun exposure (in reasonable

amounts, of course) and, for some reason, bathing in ocean water. Other treatments, such as avoidance of certain foods, allergen desensitization and stress reduction (including psychotherapy or behavior modification therapy), may provide some relief.

None of these, I should say, works very well for me.

Interestingly, when I was a kid, sun exposure healed me right up. Maddeningly, at this point in my life it is literally poison for my skin—I get sun poisoning, my entire face turning into a ruby balloon. I have also tried desensitization—trying to develop immunities to various allergens—several times. I've avoided numerous foods—I'm even vegan. And I'm pretty good, as eczema sufferers go, at dealing with emotional issues and stress. I had a masseuse who was very sympathetic and was diligent about rubbing oil into the really nasty spots. None of these has helped my skin, but the massages sure felt great.

The bad news is, for chronic, moderate-to-severe "eczematics" like me, seeking relief via more ambitious measures often carries a risk. Immunosuppressive medications such as oral and topical steroids (prednisone and hydrocortisone) will often clear things right up. The problem is that long-term use of steroids, especially taken orally, is inevitably harmful. The list of common side effects is very long and ominous, starting with infection, and skin with eczema is highly susceptible to infection anyway. Other side effects include high blood pressure, diabetes and loss of bone mass. Topical steroid preparations can permanently thin and damage skin. One of my doctors, Brian Turrisi of Washington, said, "Taking steroids is like making a pact with the devil. You will eventually pay a price."

And so I have used steroidal treatments only judiciously, in low doses or in brief bursts for bad outbreaks.

Some dermatologists use phototherapy, which combines

ultraviolet light with the drug psoralen, though this approach, like steroids, can be damaging to the skin in the long run.

Having had limited success with even more aggressive treatment, I decided to journey, like the dermatologic superhero I am, to the fringes of eczema therapy. I went to places few eczematics have gone, to places only, say, Rod Serling would have gone if he had had eczema as bad as mine.

In 1999, as my condition worsened—my eyes became very swollen and I developed abrasions on my cornea from the irritation—doctors at the University of Miami and I got bold and tried a risky therapy: cyclosporin, an immunosuppressive drug that was developed to keep transplant patients from rejecting their new organs. The idea made sense to me—my body was, in a sense, rejecting my skin (even though it was, I swear, the original skin my body came with). My dermatologist told me that one of his patients, a cruise line employee, was thrilled with the therapy. I figured if it was good for Captain Stubing, it would be good for me.

Unhappily, I made the tactical mistake of reading the cyclosporin package insert before taking the first dose. The warnings, cautions and considerations were endless. With many drugs, studies have indicated that side effects are not very common. With cyclosporin, you were almost guaranteed to get sick on the stuff: malaise, chills, fever, high blood pressure, even hirsutism (extra hair!). It was as if I were about to take uranium tailings.

Though the therapy did clear up my skin, after about six weeks I developed—you were about to guess this—fever, malaise and chills. Call me a wuss, but I didn't wait for the hirsutism to kick in, and quit taking the medication. Unfortunately, my side effects persisted even after I stopped the pills. Further testing revealed clusters of red blood cells in my urine and strange nodules on my right lung.

After two hospitalizations, many tests, surgery to biopsy my lung, and the not entirely irrational fear of cancer or tuberculosis, doctors determined that my immune system had "over-compensated" for the suppressive therapy.

But Eczema Boy, that hearty soul, was soon back at his wild explorations.

I decided to try something different and went to visit a well-credentialed, highly recommended practitioner of Chinese medicine. He was also an M.D., which gave me more confidence. Over a period of four months, we tried acupuncture and herbs, but nothing worked. Though I enjoyed the forty-five-minute sessions of acupuncture — it was actually relaxing, even with needles protruding from my hands and ankles — I got no relief from any symptoms. And because my insurance covered only about half of this expensive, time-intensive therapy, I gave it up.

Shortly after my return from Eastern medicine, I made a fortunate personal connection to the National Institutes of Health (NIH), and for absolutely no (financial) cost, I was poked and prodded by NIH ophthalmologists, immunologists and dermatologists. NIH's decision to give me a look was not part of any program, per se. I believe they did it out of empathy and medical curiosity. I was used as a teaching tool for their scholarly colleagues. I posed for a lot of pictures. I wasn't just Eczema Boy, I was an eczema poster boy!

They performed all kinds of tests, took cultures, investigated me for new life forms. And ultimately, they . . . came up with nothing new. They confirmed that, well, I had really bad eczema.

I investigated other systemic therapies, but many were experimental, and they were all immunosuppressive and carried with them a good chance of major side effects. After my dangerous dance with cyclosporin, I wasn't game.

Still not ready to hang up my cape, I revisited a promising option that my dermatologist, Arthur Ugel of Bethesda, had suggested.

Known as a topical immunomodulator — a fancy term for an immunosuppressive treatment that goes on your skin — this new ointment worked pretty well. The active ingredient, tacrolimus, is similar to cyclosporin, but in this case, I was just putting it on my skin.

It's by no means perfect — the thick ointment is uncomfortable in the summer and it can even give me a mild version of the flu-like symptoms I had on cyclosporin — but it does a decent job at keeping my skin relatively clear. And tacrolimus ointment doesn't damage or thin skin the way long-term use of steroid preparations can. However, the FDA is concerned it may increase the risk of some cancers. Most dermatologists downplay the risk. The bottom line is: No one knows for certain, so I just use the stuff judiciously and hope for something better down the road.

After many years of tough dermatologic battles, I have not given up in this scabby war. In the words of Monty Python, "I'm not dead yet! See? I have a smile on my face." I don't believe eczema is my destiny. I believe overcoming it is. I now imagine the day not too far in the future when I am at the beach, wearing only skimpy shorts and a slick film of sunscreen, surrounded by supermodels caressing my flawless skin. "But where," they will tease, "did Eczema Boy go?"

I, bronze and reckless in the bright sunshine, will smile a knowing smile.

PINK FLOYD 1977

Aired on WTMD, NPR in Baltimore (Spring 2004)

Seeing Pink Floyd for my first concert was like losing my virginity to a super model. I was sixteen-years old.

It took place on the shores of Lake Erie at Cleveland Municipal Stadium on June 25, 1977. More than 90,000 of Cleveland's finest stoners packed the place.

My buddy Jack Dempsey and I drove to the show in my mother's '70 Pontiac Catalina. I had just gotten my license, and had never driven into downtown Cleveland on my own. We brought a fifteen-piece bucket of Kentucky Fried Chicken, a cooler of Hawaiian Punch, a generous supply of reefer, and more anticipation and excitement than we could contain.

Seating was general admission, so Dempsey and I arrived at 3 p.m. for a show that didn't ultimately start until 9 p.m. We picked seats in the front row of the upper deck in right field, giving us an ideal, unobstructed view of the stage in the center field bleachers.

For the next few hours, we just sat back and watched the crowd slowly build. On the infield below us, Floyd fans were partying, playing Frisbee, food fighting, shooting off bottle rockets, and climbing the foul poles. We saw one half-naked couple making out, oblivious to the crowd enjoying their impromptu opening act.

Just before the concert was scheduled to start, a strong thunderstorm rolled through the area. Dempsey and I freaked; we were afraid the show would be cancelled, because of the intense lightning and torrential rain. But like many summer storms, this one was relatively brief, and Pink Floyd took the stage about a half hour after the skies cleared.

The trademarks of the *Animals* tour were visual: the massive helium-filled pig, inflatable human and animal props, on-stage pyrotechnics, and state-of-the-art psychedelic video footage. In what is now more than thirty years of concert-going, I've never seen such an elaborate production.

But what I remember most is the way the sound carried and echoed through the old cavernous stadium. The music came from all directions, and hung in the air like an ether. Every bend, pick and strum from David Gilmour's guitar seemed to carry without end. The background effects coming from Richard Wright's synthesizers were like a fourth dimension. The highlight of the concert was the "outro" to the song "Wish You Were Here," which is like the sound of wind whooshing through trees. For me, it was the sound of the wind in outer space. Never had I heard music that was so atmospheric and omnipresent. As we would say back then, our minds were blown.

I remember running back to the car after the show, because Dempsey and I were so pumped from the experience. I swore I heard *Dark Side of the Moon* coming from the stadium as we made or way through the streets of Cleveland. At the time, I thought it might have just been the reefer, but it occurred to me a year or two later that it was probably the encore that we had no idea was typical of most concerts. Yes, we were virgins.

The Pontiac Catalina died in '78. Roger Waters, the creative genius of Pink Floyd, left the group in '83. I lost track of Dempsey in '86. And, Cleveland Municipal Stadium was torn down in '93. But every June 25th, I make it a point to recall how in '77, the people, elements, and music came together so perfectly for my first concert experience.

DEEMED WORTHLESS

Aired on NPR's Morning Edition *(January 22, 2003)*

My brokerage firm, Charles Schwab, recently sent me a letter informing me that my 150 shares of PSINet are "deemed worthless." The fact that this Internet company's stock had plummeted to nil was not news to me. I knew for months that my PSINet shares had less value than a set of second-hand tiddly winks.

The phrase, "deemed worthless," is what caught my attention. I'm amazed that in our age of extreme marketing, rampant misinformation and corporate fraud, a company dared to be so brutally honest.

I don't imagine Ford will use the name Guzzler for their next SUV. Nor do I suspect we'll see a McDonald's burger called the McFat. "Honey, I'm going to the corner to fill up the Guzzler…again. Want me to pick up a couple of McFats for dinner?"

The fact is: Companies are inclined to be less than truthful. For instance, Sprint calls their wireless phone service "free and clear." The only thing clear is that their service is anything but free.

Admittedly, honesty can be a slippery slope. Consider Françoise Ducros, former communications director for the prime minister of Canada. She called President Bush a moron, and subsequently resigned because of the uproar it caused. Ironically, it was completely acceptable to call Dan Quayle a moron when he was vice president under President Bush, Sr.

As far as the phrase "deemed worthless" is concerned, I don't have any hard and fast rules for when it's appropriate. My ex-fiancée once deemed me worthless during couple's therapy. She got a gold star for openly expressing her feelings. Despite being deemed worthless, I still had to pay $150 for the session.

As far as the letter from Schwab is concerned, I'm looking at it as sort of a Zen experience. Short of a tax write-off, there isn't much I can do with a stock deemed worthless. I accept that reality, and I'll move on.

Like the president said during his 2000 election campaign, "…the past is over."

AN OLD YEARBOOK PROVIDES INSIGHTS INTO AN UNTOLD STORY

My grandfather died in 1985, the night before the last exam of my undergraduate career. He passed away in his sleep. I remember picking out a casket with my family in the morning, and then racing off to take my final test that afternoon.

Despite chronic high blood pressure, an irregular heartbeat, and 70-plus years of smoking, he remained relatively healthy until the final year or two of his life. We were saddened to lose Grandpa Army, but at the same time, we were glad he didn't suffer from some long debilitating illness.

Born in 1899, Army Leo Greenfield lived in Cleveland, Ohio, his entire life, and worked as a beauty supply salesman. As a young boy, I remember all the boxes of beauty paraphernalia stacked in the back seat of his car. He had a reputation for being a charmer with women, so I bet he enjoyed making rounds to all those salons inhabited by beautiful stylists.

He retired by the time I was eight, and spent his remaining years hanging out everyday with his buddies at a local diner and bowling alley. Despite his casual lifestyle, he still wore a tie, wing-tipped shoes, and fedora everyday. He still looked like he meant business.

I vaguely remember his wife, Grandma Shirley, who had suffered a massive stroke. She passed away when I was in the second grade and had been bedridden in a nursing home for many years. My grandfather visited her every day at dinnertime to feed her.

That was the extent of what I knew about Grandpa Army and his life. He was a man of few words or emotions — a model stoic you might say. More than anything, he was known for his frugality, but no one could complain too much, because his wallet was always there when someone in the family really needed help.

Grandpa Army lived with my mother and me during my high school years, but we never formed much of a relationship. When he was home in the evening, he spent many hours staring at the television through his black-rimmed, coke-bottle glasses. Maybe he'd let out a chuckle during Johnny Carson's monologue, but that was about it.

I wouldn't say Grandpa Army had given up on life, he just didn't want much from it in his later days.

Today, my mother is seventy-six and still lives in the condo the three of us shared in the late '70s. I now live in Baltimore, but every time I visit, she gives me some piece of family memorabilia. During my last trip home, she pulled out my grandfather's high school year book.

Titled "The June Bug: 1918," it's a nicely bound, 200-page book with a wonderful musty smell. Maybe most notable is the fact that it was produced by the East Technical High School print shop, and of course, long before the advent of desktop publishing. It's impressive how well the ninety-year-old book has held up, especially given that it was made by a group of high school students who literally used old-school technology. My buddies and I from the Class of '79 could barely produce a one-page typewritten essay, let alone a hardbound book.

It was surreal to see my grandfather's high school photo. He was quite a handsome young man, and his light-colored eyes, yet to be obscured by thick, post-cataract glasses, were hypnotic. I could see the same solemn expression that was to become his trademark in adulthood. The caption next to his photo read: "Here is one who need not strive to make a name for himself. He is already generously supplied." I think the quote is complimentary — I hope it is — but regardless, it isn't very revealing.

Besides the fact that he was in the electronics club, there was disappointingly no other reference to Army Leo Greenfield anywhere else in the June Bug.

However, as I perused the photos and entries in the ancient yearbook, there were a number of things that caught my attention. First of all, like my grandfather, virtually no one was smiling. Also, most of the students were quite slim; very few carried any extra weight. No one was going home after school and downing a bag of Doritos for their mid-afternoon snack.

I was intrigued by how many clubs the school had: The Palladium Society (girls honors), The East Tech Aggies (agriculture), Art Study Club, The Ben Franklin Club (printing), The Scarabaean Literary Society (boys), Kelmscot Club (literary, girls), The Friendship Club, The Chemistry Club, The Gothanian Club (architectural drawing), The Freeman Wreckers (electronics), and The Telutsa Club (knitting).

Most impressively, the East Tech football team, the Scarabs, did not give up a single point in their seven conference games in 1917. Talk about an impenetrable defense.

I managed to go my entire high school career without joining a single club. Granted, my school had far fewer clubs than East Tech, because those activities would have taken precious time from me and my friends' favorite scholastic pastime: loitering.

Perhaps most intriguing about the June Bug was that every teacher and student had their home address listed. The reason: Only about one-third of all households had phones. If you wanted to talk to somebody, you had to go to their house.

For that matter, most people didn't have cars, virtually no one had a refrigerator, and there wasn't even a licensed radio station in the whole state of Ohio.

I guess if it wasn't for all those clubs, my grandfather and his classmates would have aimlessly wandered the streets of Cleveland looking for something to do (just like I did with my buddies in the late '70s).

Not only was American society yet to have many modern conveniences in 1918, the country was immersed in World War I — The War to End All Wars — that killed 40 million, and the great flu pandemic, which killed almost 700,000 Americans and infected 28 percent of the U.S. population.

I can't begin to imagine how we'd handle such phenomena in our country today. But maybe the times in which my grandfather grew up explain why he was quiet and steady in later life. Maybe there was something about that earlier way of life he was desperately trying to hold on to: the simplicity, the humility, and the lack of expectations.

If I look at today's fast and materialistic society through the eyes of Army Leo Greenfield, the "progress" we've made, and all the economic, social, and environmental baggage that comes with it, is a mixed blessing. If nothing else, it had to be somewhat overwhelming for him.

At just the age of forty-six, even I find today's world difficult to comprehend at times. For me, the advent of Hummers, reality television, and $100 million athletes is nauseating. Yet, my iPod — a pocket-sized device that holds thousands of songs and videos — is nothing less than a piece of magic.

I do wish the June Bug had given me more details and anecdotes about my grandfather. However, the yearbook did give me a better appreciation for who he had become in later life. I finally feel like I understand him. Most surprisingly, I'm now finding remarkable virtue in his modest legacy.

COLUMNISTS CONVERGE ON PHILLY

*Appeared on www.columnists.com, the Web Site of the
National Society of Newspaper Columists (July 2007)*

In June 2007, Philadelphia became Mecca for newspaper
columnists. The City of Brotherly Love transformed into the City of
Brotherly Opinions as more than 100 editorial writers from all over
the country gathered for the Annual Conference of the National
Society of Newspaper Columnists. Guest speakers included: Dave
Barry, who was absolutely hilarious; veteran commentator Clarence
Page, who was humble and reflective; and Bill O'Reilly, the master of
antagonism, who bashed liberal media for being ideological, out of
touch, and on its deathbed. Funny, for a moment I thought he was
describing the current state of the Bush Administration.

Conference attendees were also graced by the presence
of Governor Rendell and Mayor Street. These local guys were
knowledgeable, articulate, and very enthusiastic about the city.
And just like columnists, they really enjoyed espousing all sorts of
opinions. Who knew?

In addition to discussing the column-writing business,
participants were treated to tours of many of the area's historical
attractions including: Independence Hall, the National Constitution
Center, and the USS New Jersey. Philadelphia is a fitting place to
convene columnists, because of its ties to freedom, liberty, and
protection of the First Amendment. Thanks to the events that
occurred in Philadelphia, everyone, including journalists, have the
right to voice their opinions. Heck, you can even cut someone off
mid-sentence and tell them to "sit down and shut up" if you don't

agree with them, just as O'Reilly did during his keynote address.

Though there were many Conference highlights for me, what surprised me most is how much I enjoyed walking around the city. Mayor Street talked about how walkable Philly is, and the man is right. (Please don't consider this any type of political endorsement, and even if it was, I supported Ralph Nader in the last election, and a lot of good that did him.)

During one afternoon break, I stumbled upon a beautiful little park just a few blocks from my hotel. It was a spectacular day, so I decided to just hang out on a park bench and do a little people watching. Though column writers are best known for their editorializing, we also happen to be accomplished voyeurs. You have to be good at observing things if you want to form credible opinions about them. And if you experience long bouts of laziness like I do, you learn that idleness is a great time to brush up on your voyeurism skills.

As I sat on a park bench and watched the people of Philadelphia feeding pigeons, walking their dogs, chatting with friends, or enjoying a good book, I became quite relaxed and meditative. All my cares and troubles slipped away. I had realized one of those rare moments when I was truly in the present — peaceful and anxiety-free. What a great time for a nap!

Later that evening, I learned that the park was Rittenhouse Square, named after clockmaker-astronomer David Rittenhouse — a guy known for settling the Maryland-Pennsylvania state boundary dispute between the Penns and Lord Baltimore, the namesake of my city of residence. I guess it was only fitting that a Baltimorean like me felt so comfortable lounging at Rittenhouse Square.

As I headed home down I-95 on Sunday morning, enjoying the mellow, eclectic music of the *Sleepy Hollow* show on WXPN radio, I recalled all the people, places, and events of my weekend excursion in Philadelphia. Not to sound too cliché, but I did feel the love in the City of Brotherly Love.

As for Bill O'Reilly, I can't speak for his Philadelphia experience. Unlike me, an occasional freelance commentator, he's very busy and in-demand. He probably left Philly in a hurry to get to another important gig, and didn't have time to visit historic landmarks or go for a leisurely stroll. But I bet he would have enjoyed hanging out and relaxing for a while at Rittenhouse Square. Frankly, I think Bill might become a more likeable guy if he occasionally took a moment to sit down and be quiet. Just don't let him near the pigeons.

I DON'T WANT MY MTV

Aired on WYPR, NPR in Baltimore (April 25, 2008)

In 1992, I gave up television for good. I sold my last TV to a woman named Joan. We had been dating for a little while, but there was no romantic chemistry. However, Joan did have a thing for my big Sony.

That Sony really was a behemoth of a television. I still remember lifting the massive TV into the back of Joan's station wagon. I felt like the great Russian weightlifter of the '70s, Vasily Alekseyev — straining, groaning, veins popping out of my neck. However, unlike the hulking champion, I was puny and grossly overmatched. After loading the big Sony into her car, I walked away looking like Quasimodo after a long day of bell ringing.

I decided to give up my television, because I began pursuing a master's degree in poetry. What better way than a poetry degree to catapult my career forward during the high-tech boom of the '90s? And without a TV, I had no distractions and was able to put my poetic pedal to the metal.

After I earned my degree and the poetic dust settled, I continued to stay TV-free. I enjoyed reading the newspaper, listening to public radio, and going to independent movies.

Nowadays, on the occasion when I do watch some television — while staying at a hotel, for example — I can't believe how irritating the experience has become. With the advent of characters like Bill O'Reilly, Donald Trump, Judge Judy, and Bill Maher, I feel as though the TV is attacking me. These blowhards are so loud and angry regardless of whether they are coming from the right or the left. Everyone seems to have a bug up their ass about something. Even the world's most evil terrorist, Osama bin Laden, looks relatively calm on TV when compared to most American talking heads.

Also, the speed, intensity, and frequency of commercials are overwhelming — my brain can't process the sensory overload. And, if you're a guy and you're not in the market for an SUV, beer, or an erection booster, the ads don't even apply.

When I was a kid growing up in the late '60s, I had a more symbiotic relationship with the television. First of all, you had to walk up to the TV to turn it on or change the channel. There were only three major stations, and depending on where you lived, they might not all come in clearly. I spent countless hours adjusting the fine tuning and the antennae to get a decent picture. On some sets, I had to venture to the back to get the horizontal and vertical settings right. My family had one TV that only came on "half-way" when you pulled the power knob — you had to slap the side of it to actually get a picture.

Because we had only one television set in my house, when my Grandpa Army wanted to watch *Polka Varieties* on Sunday morning, I had to endure *Polka Varieties*. I never saw the man dance a step, but my grandfather was transfixed by that weekly thirty-minute polka-thon. Fortunately, though, an afternoon baseball or football game usually followed, and we both enjoyed watching live-action sporting events.

But back then, the *Outer Limits* was my favorite program. Reruns of the show aired on Saturday afternoons when our house was quiet and empty. It always began with the words, "There's nothing wrong with your television set." That opening was ingenious, because it brought the scary program right into your home, right to the TV in front of you. The show didn't rely on high-tech special effects. The dark, spacey theme music was responsible for much of the creep factor.

Though the *Outer Limits* had some highly creative themes and characters, the episodes often involved everyday people — people like your friends or neighbors or even your parents. I'd keep to myself after watching the program, wondering who in my neighborhood might really be possessed by an alien. The *Outer Limits* is what made me ponder the possibility that I was living in a world of complete illusion — a world where I was the only real "being" and everyone and everything else was just a prop. I bet the show did a lot to boost the demand for psychotherapy. Nowadays, with shows like *Dr. Phil*, the television *is* psychotherapy.

It's too bad that today's programming has become so awful, because TV technology is quite impressive. The picture quality is spectacular, and there's little risk of a hernia when transporting these new, streamlined sets. If my grandfather were alive today, I bet I would enjoy joining him for a ballgame in crisp, clear HDTV. But then again, unless MTV gets some polka programming, it just wouldn't be the same.

A RUNNER'S JOURNEY TO YOGA

Appeared in American Health & Fitness *(April-May 2003)*

In most respects, running and yoga are at opposite ends of the exercise spectrum.

We runners go places. We ramble for many miles, over hill and dale, dressed (or undressed) to survive whatever climatic conditions mother-nature deals out. We sweat and pant to reach and ride the buzz of a mega endorphin release. I get glassy-eyed just thinking about it.

By contrast, with yoga, everything takes place on a small mat. You don't physically go anywhere. Yoga is about bending, stretching, and attempting rather odd contortions and postures named after animals. When I'm done with my practice, I feel completely loosened up, like a wrung washcloth.

As an avid runner for more than two decades who never practiced stretching, yoga continues to be quite humbling. Even after years of practice, my calves, hamstrings and quads threaten a major work stoppage each time I begin a session.

I picked up yoga during my first winter in Iowa after living in Washington, D.C., for a number of years. Continuous single-digit temperatures, strong winds and heavy snow inspired me to look for an exercise alternative indoors.

I practice two evenings a week at a place called Yoga on 5th, which I sometimes refer to as "Yoga on a 5th," postulating that a large amount of hard alcohol will help with those tougher postures.

The proprietor of Yoga on 5th, Brette, is a former gymnast and cheerleader who studied yoga intensively in California. She's about five-feet tall, and I'm convinced she's genetically linked to Gumby. Brette employs another instructor, Kelli, a friendly, unassuming young woman who holds postures long enough to impress the Marquis de Sade.

At the beginning of each session, we assume meditative and relaxing positions to bring awareness to our bodies and minds. (I take that opportunity to pray to the god of limb attachment.)

The bulk of our practice is spent repeating a flowing series of poses known as a vinyasa. The cornerstone of the vinyasa is a position called Downward-Facing Dog or simply Down Dog. (In Sanskrit, it's called Adaho Mukha Svanasana.) If you've ever seen a dog stretch its front legs, that's Downward-Facing Dog. Essentially, you get on all fours and then stick your butt high in the air while extending your arms and legs. It's not the most dignified position, but thankfully Brette guides us in proper alignment and transition, while preventing mass suffocation by reminding us to breathe. Nevertheless, Down Dog and the rest of the vinyasa is my favorite part of the practice — it has an aerobic quality and provides excellent stretching and strength building.

During the latter part of our practice, we do inversions (upside down postures). Most of those are difficult. To my amazement, though, I've managed respectable shoulder stands, headstands, handstands and back bends. Though I've made good progress, I'm not considering a Cirque du Soleil tryout anytime soon.

The continuous challenge is where yoga and running come together; for whether it's my typical five-mile run or a ninety-minute yoga session, I'm always humbled. Yes, there are occasions when I feel as though I can run forever, or a yoga practice that seems to just come to me, but those are relatively rare. Intellectually, I may know that I'll almost always complete either activity, but emotionally, there is almost always some element of doubt, of the need to prove it to myself. And, there is always another mile or a faster mile, or a new posture or a better posture.

What's more for me, whether I'm lacing up my shoes at the edge of a running path or stepping barefoot onto my mat, I know that I am embarking on a transformation. I always return from a run or a yoga practice a little different from when I started. Each encounter is a new experience for the mind, the body and the relationship between the two. Each encounter is new life.

A LESSON IN WHAT WE DON'T KNOW

Appeared in The Baltimore Sun *(December 26, 2006) and in*
Sky and Telescope Magazine *(April 2007)*

In 2006, I attended a National Association of Science Writers Conference in Baltimore, which offered "Lunch with a Scientist" — a menu of informal talks on a wide range of topics. Though my employer pays me to know and write about the retina — the thin piece of vision-critical tissue in the back of the eye — I decided to be a little derelict in my duties and learn about something completely new and unrelated.

I considered sitting at the table where "Breaking Up is Hard to Do: Lessons from an Amoeba" was being presented, but I figured that might lead to flashbacks of former girlfriends and images of pond scum—two topics that don't exactly arouse my appetite.

Instead, I decided to hang out where "Dark Energy and the History of Cosmic Expansion" was being discussed. Maybe I listened to a little too much Pink Floyd in high school, but anything cosmic grabs my attention, and I knew that the relatively new concept of dark energy was blowing away even the best astronomical minds.

Adam Riess, Ph.D., from Johns Hopkins University was the cosmic expert who gave our table of eight the lowdown on dark energy. Riess was intense and focused. It was clear to me that while I was in college, busy searching for the next party or rock concert, he was busy searching the skies for astronomical wonders.

Riess began his lunchtime talk by explaining that dark energy is this highly abundant stuff out in space that is causing our universe to expand. It seems to balance well with equally mysterious dark matter, creating a sort of a cosmic yin-yang. Beyond that, we don't know a whole lot more. We're not sure what dark energy and dark matter are, exactly; we only know they are dark, and they affect the movement of cosmic objects. Also, we don't know how long the universe will keep expanding, what will happen if it stops expanding, and whether there are other universes out there.

I was blown away even before I finished my appetizer, struck by the realization that when it comes right down to it, we don't know how the heck we got here, nor do we know where we're going.

But Riess was just getting warmed up. He went on to talk about the "Anthropic Principle," which offers an explanation of why all the constants and forces of the universe happen to work just right to support cosmic harmony and life on our planet. If there were just minor deviations in the strength of gravity, or the weight of protons or neutrons in atoms, our universe wouldn't have held up. Also, if ice didn't float, our oceans would freeze from the bottom up and the surface of the Earth would be frozen.

Of course, those who profess creationism or intelligent design think they have the answer to why things in universe worked out so well, but for the hard-core scientists looking for a scientific explanation, the Anthropic Principle is one possibility. The Anthropic Principle suggests that we — our universe and everything in it — are lucky. That is, there have been a zillion big bangs, and the one that created our universe, with all its nicely coordinated constants and forces, just happened to work out. We hit the cosmic lottery.

Keep in mind that the Anthropic Principle is a theory, and the guys who proposed this idea don't suggest that it is anything more. Maybe someday, new discoveries will support or refute this supposition.

Riess concluded his discussion by giving each of us a photo he had taken using the Hubble Space Telescope. I got a great, glossy picture of Spiral Galaxy NGC 3370. (I shudder to think what the people at the amoeba table got as parting gifts.)

Though I was thrilled to learn so many new things about the cosmos, I was equally impressed to hear about all the things we don't know. At a time when our political leaders and the media espouse so much certainty about virtually everything, it was refreshing to hear an intelligent, level-headed guy acknowledge all the stuff we don't know. That hour-long lunch helped me appreciate the beauty of the mystery we live in. Isn't that one of the great things about being a human on this Earth—to wonder, search and discover?

Einstein put it well when he said, "The most beautiful thing we can experience is the mysterious. It is the source of all true art and all science. He to whom this emotion is a stranger, who can no longer pause to wonder and stand rapt in awe, is as good as dead: His eyes are closed."

SENIOR READING GROUP GETS COSMIC

When I first volunteered to read to the residents of a retirement home in Iowa, I happened to pick a rather graphic Dave Barry essay on childbirth. Three ladies stomped off in complete disgust, never to return to my group again. I think the passage about the doctor holding up the placenta is what got them running for the exits. Or maybe the story brought back bad memories of frontier anesthesiology.

In any case, hoping to find a safer topic, I recently selected an article on the dawn of the cosmos. I figured a discussion of the birth of our universe was less personal and slimy than births involving umbilical cords, c-sections, and dilating cervixes.

However, when I read that the universe has 100 billion galaxies, each with billions of stars, I suddenly felt completely insignificant and meaningless. And, I didn't think this was what people in the twilight of their lives wanted to try to comprehend. In the back of my mind, I could hear the familiar '70s song lyric "All we are is dust in the wind."

I knew the universe was big, but the math was mind-blowing: 100 billion galaxies, each with billions of stars? Heck, Bingo only goes up to seventy. I could have used a cosmic intervention from Carl Sagan.

I paused to see how the group was reacting. To my right, ninety-five-year-old Vern was staring off in the distance, probably fantasizing about one of the other 99 billion galaxies in the universe. Bob, to my left, did raise an eyebrow, but for all I knew, it was because his Ex-Lax had just kicked in. Burl, still aglow from his 100th birthday earlier in the week, pointed to me and said, "You're OK with me young man."

Everyone else sat in silence, so I kept going.

Further along in the story, I read how the Andromeda galaxy and our galaxy, the Milky Way, were hurdling toward each other at 300,000 miles per hour. A slight, soft-spoken woman named Catherine turned to me and asked, "So what's gonna happen?" I had good news. Andromeda won't reach us for billions of years!

At the end of reading group, everyone got up from the table and shuffled off, some in wheel chairs — others pulling canes and walkers. As always, they thanked me for visiting, and I thanked them for joining me. Though I always leave the home with a sense of humility, I felt particularly humbled on that Sunday. The cosmic journey may have rattled me, but they took it all in stride.

I was glad knowing that when Andromeda does come precariously close to us in a billion years, it'll be some other reader who'll need to explain the outcome to a different group of seniors.

For now, I think we'll all be satisfied if we just make it back to reading group next week.

A LONG LOST LIFE SLIPS INTO FOCUS
Appeared in The Washington Post *(March 26, 2007)*

Over the past few years, my mother has been sending me
an odd assortment of nostalgic items including my Cub Scout
neckerchief, first-grade report card, and great grandparents'
naturalization papers. In one envelope was a black and white photo
of my father circa 1960. He was about thirty-years old then, newly
married to my mother. I arrived on the scene about a year later. My
mother could have been pregnant with me when the photo was
taken, or maybe they were just in the planning stages. "Honey, let's
have a baby."

At that moment in time, he was still just Stan, not yet having
achieved dad status. Stan was a plumber and looked just like one in
the picture; a short stocky guy with glasses dressed in a flannel shirt,
work pants, and a cap. He's standing with his hands in the pockets
of his jacket, and smiling with a cigarette between his lips. Back
then, people enjoyed smoking. It wasn't just a habit, it was a look. I
can imagine Stan saying, "Wait. Let me light up a Camel before you
take that shot."

My parents decided to divorce in 1963, the same year Kennedy
was shot. They were having financial problems, because my dad
wasn't working. My mother had to drop me off at a friend's house
during the day so she could work in the medical records department
of a hospital. Eventually, they couldn't make payments on their
house. What a year for the Shabermans.

I have virtually no memory of my mother and father ever being together. The only recollection I do have is muddled. I can't attest to its validity. It could have easily been a moment in a dream. What I remember is standing in a crib in a bedroom while my parents were arguing. They were in their underwear. I never bothered asking if they kept my crib in the bedroom or if they liked to prance around in their skivvies.

After the divorce, neither of my parents ever remarried or dated much. I lived with my mother and saw my dad on occasional weekends, when we were living in the same town. We'd go to the movies, bowling, and fishing. My dad was a wealth of knowledge and enjoyed rattling on about all sorts of facts, people, and events, even if I had no interest in who or what he was talking about. We would sometimes visit a friend or a relative, and he was invariably asked to repair something — a washer, toilet, or furnace. My dad could fix anything, though he loved to toy with people when he was working. He'd be wedged under the kitchen sink of some stressed-out housewife and proclaim, "Ya, I think we'll need to re-do the plumbing for the whole house," only to emerge a few minutes later having easily fixed the problem.

My dad and I had a falling out when I was sixteen, because he was angry with my rebellious lifestyle and the fact I was not doing well in school. He was convinced I'd never amount to anything, and it broke his heart. We didn't talk for seven years. I reconnected with him during my last year of college. He died from lung cancer just after I graduated.

The last time I saw my dad, he was on a ventilator in the intensive care unit at a hospital. Through a series of hand motions and scribblings on a piece of paper, he was able to let me know that there was some cash in a drawer in his apartment that he wanted me to take. I found the money. He died a few days later.

My mother admitted to me recently that she had never loved my father. She just wanted a child, she said. I had suspected this all along, because of information I pieced together over the years. Though my dad would have never admitted it, I think he loved her.

I'm drawn to that old photo of my father, because it captures such a happy moment in his life. Young Stan had a new wife and a baby on the way. The future was quite hopeful. And though I wish he could be here with me now, how great it must have been to have known him then.

ACKNOWLEDGMENTS

I would like to thank the following people who helped make
The Vegan Monologues possible:

Jeannie McStay

Gregg Wilhelm

Kevin Atticks

KK Ludwig-Lapper

Lena Ludwig-Lapper

Keryl Cryer

Katie Giblin

Chelsea Leiner

Davida Gypsy Brier

Nicholas Marx

Jennifer Bridges

Aaron Henkin

David Pace

Carrie Mattson

ABOUT THE AUTHOR

Ben Shaberman's essays have appeared in the *Chicago Tribune*, *Baltimore Sun*, *Vegetarian Times*, *VegNews*, and a variety of other publications, including the *Washington Post*, which says Shaberman is "undaunted by the white-coated villains who insist he is beyond help." His commentaries have also been carried by NPR's *Morning Edition*, as well as NPR in Baltimore and Des Moines. He earned a master's degree in poetry from Johns Hopkins University, and is a member of the National Society of Newspaper Columnists. Shaberman lives in Baltimore and can be found at www.benshaberman.com.

The future of publishing...today!

Apprentice House is the country's only campus-based, student-staffed book publishing company. Directed by professors and industry professionals, it is a nonprofit activity of the Communication Department at Loyola College in Maryland.

Using state-of-the-art technology and an experiential learning model of education, Apprentice House publishes books in untraditional ways. This dual responsibility as publishers and educators creates an unprecedented collaborative environment among faculty and students, while teaching tomorrow's editors, designers, and marketers.

Outside of class, progress on book projects is carried forth by the AH Book Publishing Club, a co-curricular campus organization supported by Loyola College's Office of Student Activities.

Student Project Team for *The Vegan Monologues*:

>Katie Giblin, '08

>Chelsea Leiner, '08

>Nicholas Marx, '09

>Stephanie Meros, '09

To learn more about Apprentice House books or to obtain submission guidelines, please visit www.ApprenticeHouse.com.

Apprentice House
Communication Department
Loyola College in Maryland
4501 N. Charles Street
Baltimore, MD 21210
Ph: 410-617-5265
Fax: 410-617-5040
info@apprenticehouse.com

CPSIA information can be obtained at www.ICGtesting.com
Printed in the USA
LVOW01s1958131213

365204LV00003B/227/P

9 781934 074367